The Oxford Poetry Library

GENERAL EDITOR: FRANK KERMODE

GEORGE GORDON was born in London on 22 January 1788. On his mother's side he was Scottish of French extraction; his father's family was ancient and noble, and came to England with William the Conqueror. He was born with a deformed right foot. With the death of the Fifth Baron Byron of Rochdale early in 1798, and in default of nearer heirs, he succeeded to the title. As Lord Byron he was soon to become the most famous poet of his age, as well as one of its most celebrated, if not notorious, characters. His career spans a momentous period in European history in which Byron himself was deeply involved. The crucial dates in this career are 1812, when he rocketed to fame with the publication of *Childe Harold*; 1816, when his marriage failed and he left England; and 1824, when he died in Missolonghi, Greece, where he had gone to join the forces struggling for Greek independence.

JEROME J. McGANN is the John Stewart Bryan Professor of English, University of Virginia. He has published widely on nineteenth- and twentieth-century literature, and is the editor of Byron's *Complete Poetical Works* (in seven volumes) and *The New Oxford Book of Romantic Period Verse*.

FRANK KERMODE, retired King Edward VII Professor of English Literature at Cambridge, is the author of many books, including *Romantic Image, The Sense of an Ending, The Classic, The Genesis of Secrecy, Forms of Attention,* and *History and Value;* he is also co-editor with John Hollander of *The Oxford Anthology of English Literature.*

THE OXFORD POETRY LIBRARY

GENERAL EDITOR: FRANK KERMODE

Matthew Arnold	*Miriam Allott*
William Blake	*Michael Mason*
Byron	*Jerome J. McGann*
Samuel Taylor Coleridge	*Heather Jackson*
John Dryden	*Keith Walker*
Thomas Hardy	*Samuel Hynes*
George Herbert	*Louis Martz*
Gerard Manley Hopkins	*Catherine Phillips*
Ben Jonson	*Ian Donaldson*
John Keats	*Elizabeth Cook*
Andrew Marvell	*Frank Kermode and Keith Walker*
John Milton	*Jonathan Goldberg and Stephen Orgel*
Alexander Pope	*Pat Rogers*
Sir Philip Sidney	*Katherine Duncan-Jones*
Henry Vaughan	*Louis Martz*
William Wordsworth	*Stephen Gill and Duncan Wu*

The Oxford Poetry Library

Byron

Edited by
JEROME J. McGANN

Oxford   New York
OXFORD UNIVERSITY PRESS
1994

Oxford University Press, Walton Street, Oxford OX2 6DP

Oxford New York Toronto
Delhi Bombay Calcutta Madras Karachi
Kuala Lumpur Singapore Hong Kong Tokyo
Nairobi Dar es Salaam Cape Town
Melbourne Auckland Madrid
and associated companies in
Berlin Ibadan

Oxford is a trade mark of Oxford University Press

This selection first published in The Oxford Poetry Library 1994

British Library Cataloguing in Publication Data
Data available

Library of Congress Cataloging in Publication Data
Byron, George Gordon, Baron, 1788–1824.
[Selections. 1994]
Byron / edited by Jerome J. McGann.
p. cm. — (The Oxford poetry library)
Includes bibliographical references and indexes.
i. McGann, Jerome J. II. Title. III. Series.
PR4353.M38 1994 821'.7—dc20 93–30409
ISBN 0–19–282267–5

1 3 5 7 9 10 8 6 4 2

Typeset by Rowland Phototypesetting Ltd
Printed in Great Britain by
Biddles Ltd
Guildford and King's Lynn

Contents

Introduction

I

Byron was born in London the year before the French Revolution broke out in Paris in 1789; he died in Greece in 1824. Since that time, students of history and literature have often dated the Romantic Period 1789–1824, partly because the character of this period was so determined by the epochal events in France, and partly because the career of Byron seemed at once its summary and its climax. No other literary figure, not even Goethe, was so widely and actively engaged with the important people and events of his time. Unlike Wordsworth, who stands with Byron as pre-eminent among the great English poets of the period, Byron was a European writer and (if the pun be permitted) man of affairs. Everything he wrote established explicit filiations with the world in which he moved, and his work sought, in addition, to see and represent the historical patterns and continuities which connected the present to the recent and distant past. Byron's work is, in every sense, a poetry of experience.

From his earliest to his latest work, however, the experiences which underpin both the deeds and the ideas of Byron's literary work assume a peculiar and characteristic form. Byron writes himself into all his poetry, of course, but the self thus represented is always viewed in a detailed context of impinging social and historical relations. More, Byron insists—increasingly so as his career unfolds—that the context which envelops his life is of world-historical dimensions. This quality of his work is reflected in all its material aspects: in the sweeping range of its topics, subjects, and models (classical and European alike, ancient and modern, English and Continental); in its deliberate embrace of the most traditional and the most experimental poetic forms; and finally in the range of the styles which he not only used, but also took seriously—from the most ephemeral types of street songs, ballads, and *vers de société* to the heroic manner of the tales, the high rhetoric of the satires, and the noble numbers of poems like *Childe Harold's Pilgrimage*. In the end—that is to say, in *Don Juan*—he reinvented, for a changing Western culture, a new high style in poetry that answered to the variegated and dynamic (not to say chaotic and unstable) social circumstances of what we now call the Modern World. Like Heine, Pushkin, and Baudelaire after him—all poets quite conscious of the tradition they had chosen—Byron's masterpiece spoke in a new *vulgaris eloquentia*.

Byron was deeply interested in poetic traditions and the place he occupied within them. We see this very clearly throughout *Don Juan* and *Childe Harold's Pilgrimage*, and it is explicit in the Dedication to the former and the opening stanzas to Canto IV of the latter. But more than his place in the temple of poetic fame, Byron was interested in his place in world history, and—more particularly and more immediately—in the *mission* which he believed he was fated to accomplish. Not every reader responds sympathetically to this grand, even theatrical way in which Byron conceives and represents himself (though few resist, or even try to resist, the *Don Juan* manner of his theatricality). Nevertheless, it is crucial to understand that all of Byron's poetry, even the work which might appear trivial, is self-conceived in a vast, and finally in a heroic, frame of reference. All of his heroes, we know, are surrogates of himself, more or less displaced. They are, as well, figures moving under the domination of an often obscure purpose and destiny. Manfred's life is ruled by his 'star', and it is thus that Byron understands and represents himself in his work. This quality has been aptly called Byron's 'need of fatality'. It lies at the heart of his entire life's work, and it achieves its greatest expression in his greatest poem, *Don Juan*.

To understand the fate which Byron needed, and which he then generated to answer that need, we have to see the human world in which he imagined himself to exist; for it is that world which his poetry half perceives and half creates.

II

When Wordsworth recalls, in *The Prelude*, the period in which his youthful imagination was nurtured, he narrates a series of benevolences and wonders. These culminate in his experience of the early years of the French Revolution when, Wordsworth says, Europe— that is to say, the new Europe whose promise seemed to be dawning—'was thrilled with joy, | France standing on the top of the golden hours, | And human nature seeming born again' (*Prelude*, VI. 339–41). Subsequent events would overbear Wordsworth's correspondent sense of joy, and force him to internalize the human promise of his early, socialized imagination of this new dawn.

Wordsworth's career as a poet is thus founded in a set of 'golden hours': not just the early years of the French Revolution, but the immediately previous years as well when, according to the myth of his life that he formulated for himself, Wordsworth grew up in the benevolent embrace of nature.

For Byron, however, the time when his imagination's eye began to see the world, the first decade of the nineteenth century, was a dark time. All of Europe was embroiled in the struggle with France, whose revolution had fallen to the hands of the brilliant and ambitious Napoleon. As First Consul and then as Emperor, Napoleon reconstituted the social structure of France and aimed at the transformation of the political structure of all Europe. His chief adversary in this struggle was England, though all the European powers were involved in various ways and degrees. Between 1801 and 1809 the situation was peculiarly ambiguous and volatile, with complex alliances and coalitions being formed between the different European states, only to be dismantled, and replaced by other arrangements. These are the years in which Napoleon's career reached its zenith—years marked by many of his outstanding military exploits, on one hand, and by a series of remarkable diplomatic and political manœuvres on the other.

Byron's first book, a privately printed volume called *Fugitive Pieces*, was produced late in 1806, for private circulation. The book cultivates preciosity and inconsequence: a loose collection of largely wretched verse—school exercises, mostly, or sentimental poems celebrating Byron's female amours and male friends. The one distinctive quality of the book is its extreme, if affected, self-consciousness; yet the one subject about which Byron is *not* self-conscious is the current state of European affairs, and England's part in these momentous events. It is as if *Fugitive Pieces* had been produced as a resort from the larger English and European scene. The book's audience, like its topics and human subjects, is located either in Cambridge or the tight Midlands society of Southwell.

In the next year and a half—that is, between late 1806 and March 1808—Byron revised and expanded his first book three times: first, as another privately printed volume called *Poems on Various Occasions* (January 1807), and then in his first two published works, *Hours of Idleness* (June 1807) and *Poems Original and Translated* (March 1808). These books extend the autobiographical structure of *Fugitive Pieces* both internally and externally. The added poems either fill out Byron's self-portrait and the context of his life (a number of the poems are explicit comments on earlier poems, as well as on the reactions which those poems had caused among friends and enemies), and the book as a whole reaches out for a wider audience—in particular, reaches out to London and the centres of English culture.

The result of Byron's effort to make contact with a larger public was something more than he had expected. *Hours of Idleness* was reviewed in the influential *Edinburgh Review* (January 1808) in a scathing *ad hominem* fashion. Though Byron at the time believed the review had been written by the chief editor Francis Jeffrey, it was actually the work of Henry Brougham, the reformist lawyer and politician who would later incur Byron's implacable hatred for other reasons entirely. This famous review is important in the history of Byron's work and career for a number of reasons. In the first place, it was the impetus behind the publication of Byron's first major poem, *English Bards and Scotch Reviewers* (March 1809). Secondly, it exposed a number of the contradictions which Byron experienced and registered in himself and in his society alike.

The production of a work like *English Bards and Scotch Reviewers* was an act of enormous pretension for a person who had barely reached his majority. Nevertheless, we now must see it as the all but inevitable conclusion of the process which Byron had set in motion when he first issued *Fugitive Pieces*: for the latter's coy self-consciousness led to the even more personal and self-conscious *Hours of Idleness*, which in turn produced the *Edinburgh Review*'s ridiculing notice, the impetus behind Byron's broad-ranging critique of English letters and culture in 1808. Byron woke up to find himself world-famous in 1812, when *Childe Harold's Pilgrimage. A Romaunt* was published, but this later event had been amply prepared by the publication of his satire three years earlier and by the immediate aftermath of that publication. Three more (authorized) editions of *English Bards* were produced between 1809 and 1811.

Byron's satire thus served to extend even further the social context in which he insisted upon asserting and defining himself. In so doing, however, Byron was forced to confront English society in a much larger frame of reference, and to deal with a number of contradictions of which he had scarcely been aware. When he wrote his early poetry Byron's closest circles and sympathies were reformist and Whig. Thus, it was a peculiar shock to find himself made an object of ridicule in the *Edinburgh Review*. When he struck back, he found his readiest weapons were often supplied by the reactionary *Anti-Jacobin* and by conservative literary voices like William Gifford. As a consequence, the most notable quality of *English Bards and Scotch Reviewers* is the peculiar and idiosyncratic nature of its social critique. Byron singles out a few *individuals* for praise and honour, but his attack is launched at the culture as a whole, where he is able to see no party, no class, no institution with which to identify. English culture is represented in a state of crisis, and Byron is but a voice crying in its wilderness.

With the publication of his satire Byron completed his plans for leaving England. This famous trip to the Peninsula and finally to the Turkish dominions in the Levant produced his equally famous account of that trip, the first two cantos of *Childe Harold*, which he published after he returned in July 1811. Here, for the first time, Byron projected his sense of social and cultural crisis to include the whole of Europe. The focus of his analysis is of course an English one, but his is an English view that has transcended the chauvinist patriotic interpretations of European affairs which were current and common in England at the time. With this book, in fact, all the most basic lines of Byron's thinking, if not the conclusions of that thinking, are set in place. It is important, therefore, to see very clearly the context which stands behind, and receives expression in, this famous publication.

As an Englishman sympathizing with the republican and reformist movements set in motion by the French Revolution, Byron was deeply ambivalent about his country's antagonistic relation to France. Unlike Wordsworth or Coleridge, for example, Byron responded to the European situation from a point of departure nearer the turn of the century than the outbreak of the Revolution a decade earlier. Because of this, Byron did not find it natural to locate the source of his period's evils and dislocations in the Reign of Terror, and hence in France's 'betrayal' of her own cause. People like Wordsworth and Coleridge saw England as the last reliable defence against French imperialism and the total destruction of the social fabric of Europe. But from Byron's later vantage the situation appeared very different. What Byron saw was a history of growing reaction against the goals of the Revolution. Increasingly Britain found herself compelled to lead the defence of ancient and entrenched European privilege—to form alliances abroad that appeared to dishonour her traditional ideals of freedom and liberty, and to repress at home, in England and Ireland, various actual struggles to express or implement those ideals. And, in the pursuit of these ends, the spokesmen for English policies resorted to what Byron saw as a canting and hypocritical denunciation of France and justification of English moves. Byron's ambivalence was further complicated by the charismatic presence of Napoleon, both in his vision of a republican transformation of Europe, and in his actual display of tactical and strategic genius in political and military affairs alike.

This disturbed and disturbing view of his own country's ideals and policies first came into unmistakable focus for Byron in the summer of 1807 when England seized the Danish fleet and bombarded Copenhagen. A truce was arranged, but in 1808 England once again betrayed Denmark by supporting a Swedish invasion with an expeditionary force of twelve thousand troops under Sir John Moore. The Whig Opposition raised an outcry, and the whole set of events involved a serious moral setback for English policies both at home and abroad. Byron himself first explicitly denounced these events in his poetry in 1811, in the mordant satiric attack privately printed in 1812 as *The Curse of Minerva*. The ostensible subject of this poem is Lord Elgin's efforts to save (or maraud) the Parthenon sculptures. In fact, the satire culminates in a wholesale denunciation of British policy, in Europe (including the Peninsula and Denmark), in Ireland, in the Levant, and even in India.

But it was the first two cantos of *Childe Harold* which articulated Byron's most compelling and most comprehensive analysis of this social and political situation. The two principal loci of Byron's travel poem are the Peninsula, where the latest phase of the struggle between France and the allied forces led by England had erupted, and the Levant—Greece, in particular—where Byron went to escape the depressing theatre of European affairs, and perhaps to rediscover for the present and for himself the source and basis of Europe's most cherished social and cultural ideals. What he found instead was, in the Peninsular War, a mere nest of vipers, and in the East the debasement of European culture. This debasement appeared most graphically in the hallowed places of ancient Greece, which Byron saw as having been inherited and inhabited by unworthy people. These included the supine Greeks themselves and their Turkish overlords, as well as the opportunistic and self-serving Europeans who maintained their interests in the area—that is, the English, the French, and the Russians. Thus the current

state of Greece became for Byron the very symbol of the current
state of European culture at large.

When Byron embodied and published this negative and critical
assessment in 1812, he achieved an all but instant celebrity through-
out England and Europe. Later readers have occasionally conde-
scended to the fame Byron reaped with *Childe Harold's Pilgrimage.
A Romaunt*, but the book is a signal and important event both in
social and in literary history. In one stroke Byron defined and
reflected back to the people of England and all Europe a crucial
insight into the meaning of the age, into the human significance of
the momentous events which were even then taking place. The
book had found a means to focus and isolate, in a tangible way, the
complex and obscure patterns of events which were affecting so
many individual lives and social structures at the time. More than
this, the book argued that what was most deplorable about living
at such a time was to be measured in terms of the individual's life.
Europe was tearing itself apart from England to the Caucasus, but
that spectacle of political ruin was no more than an expression of
what was truly to be lamented: the suffering which it brought to
the lives of individual persons. The bleeding heart which Byron
trailed across Europe became the expression of an epochal experi-
ence only because it was first and fundamentally the expression of
a single identifiable person.

The first two cantos of *Childe Harold* are also important because
of the character of the person who delivers its message. The Childe,
Byron's surrogate, is, like his creator Byron, not merely culturally
and socially disaffected; he is *young, privileged*, and also disaffected.
This is an important aspect of the book since it deepens the poem's
message of despair. That the hero is experiencing sorrow in his
youth projects an image of a desperate future, while the privilege
of his circumstances, in every sense, tells us that the social body
has been wounded even in its most protected areas. Furthermore,
Byron's decision to use symbolic forms, including fictive characters,
as slightly displaced figures of himself *in propria persona* was to have
a profound significance on the entire future course of Western
literary work. In more immediate terms, this Romantic emphasis
on the personality of the poet was to become one of the hallmarks
of all of Byron's own poetry.

III

We date Byron's so-called Years of Fame from the publication of *Childe Harold* in 1812, and we set the term of those years in April 1816, when he left England under a cloud of public disapprobation and complex suspicions. This is perhaps the best-known period of Byron's life. It is certainly the most notorious. During these years Byron moved at the centre of the most fashionable circles of Regency society. These are the years in which he wrote and published his celebrated sequence of 'Byronic Tales', those gloomy and fast-moving adventure stories most of which are set in the Levant. Like the first two cantos of *Childe Harold*, these poems sold thousands of copies in edition after edition, and they made Byron's name a household word throughout Europe. He was lionized and adulated and even adored, and he responded to his circumstances with a mixture of wonder, enthusiasm, and revulsion. These are the years of some of his most famous amours—Lady Caroline Lamb, Lady Oxford, Lady Frances Wedderburn Webster—as they are also the years in which he met, courted, and finally married the brilliant and priggish Annabella Milbanke. It was a marriage made in hell, reaping, in the end, little but wormwood and recrimination. These are also the years in which his love for his half-sister Augusta Leigh was consummated.

Byron's fast personal life and remarkable literary career during these years have tended to overshadow the social significance of these events, as well as the political geography in which the events took place and of which they are at once a function and an expression. We do not always remember that Byron's earliest determination was to pursue a public and political career rather than a life in letters. He stated this explicitly, not to say melodramatically, even in the Preface to *Hours of Idleness*. When he returned from his trip to the East in 1811 he spent several months arranging certain personal affairs and seeing to the publication of *Childe Harold*. At that point, in January 1812, Byron appeared in the House of Lords at the opening of the new session of Parliament. When he first took his seat, in 1809, shortly before his journey to the East, Byron had said that he intended to stand apart from both parties. This decision reflected what we have already seen, Byron's troubled sense that all his political and ideological alternatives were unacceptable. By 1812, however, he had acknowledged to himself that, whatever else was uncertain or unclear, he was, at any rate, of the devil's party and in opposition. As he prepared to deliver his maiden speech in the Lords, he determined to make his position as clear as possible.

He chose, for this purpose, to speak against a government-proposed bill which called for the death penalty for frame-breaking. Byron took great pains with the preparation of this speech, and he consulted with the leader of the Moderate Whigs, Lord Holland, about his ideas and his purposes. In fact, however, what Byron wanted to say—what, in the end, he *did* say in his speech—represented not a Whig but a Radical point of view. 'My own motive for opposing the bill', he told Holland, 'is founded on its palpable injustice, and its certain inefficacy. I have seen the state of these miserable men [the frame-breakers], and it is a disgrace to a civilized country.' Byron expatiated on these themes in his speech in February 1812 and his rhetoric took an inflammatory turn which was absent from his letters to Holland: 'How can you carry the Bill into effect? Can you commit a whole country to their own prisons? Will you erect a gibbet in every field, and hang up men like scarecrows?' This last image was peculiarly ironical and telling since it deliberately recalled France and the days of the Terror.

The argumentative forthrightness of Byron's maiden speech, if one were to take the text merely by itself, might easily obscure the ambivalence which lies at its heart. That Byron should have taken Holland as a confidant during its preparation indicates the sort of contradictions which Byron was experiencing. Furthermore, Byron delivered the speech with what was recognized as—with what he himself acknowledged as—'a sort of modest impudence'; and in the immediate aftermath, though he served on the committee which amended the bill by substituting fine or imprisonment for the death penalty, he did little to develop a constituency outside Parliament or a coalition within. In short, he did nothing practical or serious to implement his ideas in an institutional or political way. Byron was a Radical, but he was also a Dandy (in both the social and the Baudelairean senses), and Lord Holland's comments on his speech tell an important truth about it and Byron's politics at the time: 'His speech was full of fancy, wit, and invective, but not exempt from affectation or well reasoned, nor at all suited to our common notions of Parliamentary eloquence. His fastidious and artificial taste and his over-irritable temper would, I think, have prevented him from ever excelling in Parliament.' Holland was right, and Byron's own actions show that he knew all this as well.

Byron's plunge into the high life of Regency fashion during the next few years must be understood against the background of his desperate political ideals, on the one hand, and the actual institutional options which Byron saw before him, on the other. It is as if Byron had thrown the dice in this parliamentary game in order to prove to himself what he knew all along, that it was a gambling situation and that he was fated to lose. He wrote his tales at this time, he said, to 'hold off' certain painful realities which haunted his mind. We have always taken those 'realities' to be the complex personal relations of his love life, and in particular the anxieties which he must have experienced because of his illicit love for his sister. In addition, however, Byron's mind was haunted by certain other Ideal attachments which were connected with his social and political aims, for the famous tales of this period constitute a series of displaced meditations on the political and ideological problems which Europe, because of its history, was currently having to face. *The Giaour* is, at one level, a virtual allegory of Europe's betrayal of its most cherished political ideals, and the later tales all treat similar themes. Dominant in them is the idea that recent forces of change are bound to an ultimately ineffectual struggle with entrenched power, and that the tragic curve of these conflicts is determined by historical factors over which the present seems to have no control. The fatality of these historical factors is typically represented as a mysterious crime dogging the life of the Byronic Hero. Byron's gloomy sense of Europe's social and political prospects is dramatized in the doom of his famous heroes, but it is explicit in his Journal of 1813–14, as it is in the following epigram he spilled into a letter to Lady Melbourne:

> 'Tis said *Indifference* marks the present time,
> Then hear the reason—though 'tis told in rhyme—
> A King who *can't*—a Prince of Wales who *don't*—
> Patriots who *shan't*, and Ministers who *won't*—
> What matters who are *in* or *out* of place
> The *Mad*—the *Bad*—the *Useless*—or the *Base*?

IV

Such nihilist views help to explain not only Byron's furious pursuit of distraction and pleasure during his Years of Fame, but his persistent attempts to get himself married. The prospect of having a wife and domestic circumstances seemed to him, as it seemed to his

friends at the time, perhaps the surest way out of the vicious and
dangerous circles in which his career seemed to be moving. In 1814
he proposed to and was accepted by Anne Isabella Milbanke, the
only daughter of Sir Ralph Milbanke and Lady Judith Noel Mil-
banke, and they were married on 2 January 1815.

The foolishness of this union was not long in making itself appar-
ent. The marriage and the subsequent separation comprise a fascin-
ating and terrible story that has been told many times. Here we
need only recall its most famous consequence, the departure of
Byron from England in April 1816 amid a whirlpool of private
gossip and newspaper scandal. Public opinion, which had wor-
shipped at Byron's shrine for almost four years, now seemed to
decide that his personal life and political views were not fascinating
but simply scandalous.

Byron never returned to England. In 1816 he went first to
Switzerland, where he formed an important friendship with Shelley,
and then on to Italy, where he lived in various places for most of
the rest of his life. These years—1817–23—saw the beginning
of the European settlement under the leadership, not to say the
domination, of England. The revolutionary epoch had ended in
1815 with the notorious Congress of Vienna, the formation of the
so-called Holy Alliance, and the restoration of the European mon-
archies. In the subsequent years—that is to say, until the eruption
of civil war in Spain in 1822 and the French invasion in 1823,
England and the restored powers were preoccupied with the estab-
lishment of stable and conservative political structures and the total
eradication of revolutionary elements.

For his part, these were the years in which Byron declared him-
self 'born for opposition'. Having exiled himself from England, he
moved further and further into a critical relation with the dominant
powers of contemporary Europe and their ideologies. All his poeti-
cal work during these, his most important years, was directed
against what he called the 'cant political, cant poetical, and cant
moral' of the English and European worlds. *Don Juan* is, of course,
the culminant result of these efforts—a conscious attempt to
explain critically the meaning of the entire period in Europe stretch-
ing from 1789 to 1823.

During his initial years as expatriate bard and hero Byron was
chiefly occupied with reorienting himself to his alien cultural sur-
roundings. This process of socialization took the amusing and
highly characteristic form of a series of notorious amours. The last

of these was the liaison he formed in 1819 with the young Contessa Teresa Guiccioli (*née* Gamba). This was Byron's 'Last Attachment'. The Contessa eventually left her husband and lived with Byron until he departed from Italy in 1823 for Greece and his death. These are also the years in which he rediscovered the importance of the traditions of Italian poetry, and in which he gradually rebuilt the radical political attachments which had been left in ruins in 1814–15.

The watershed year in Byron's Italian sojourn was 1820. At this point he had settled to (but not *in*to) his new way of life, and his affair with La Guiccioli brought a degree of emotional stability which seems to have released him from an excessive self-absorption. In the middle of the year he began attending meetings of secret political societies which were agitating for Italian freedom. His involvement with this movement, through the Gambas (Teresa's father and brother), so embroiled him with the Austrian police authorities that he was eventually forced to leave Ravenna and move to Pisa, in 1821. Meantime, as the political climate in Europe grew increasingly volatile, Byron in turn grew more determined to wage ideological war with the forces of political and cultural reaction. The years 1820–3 are thus marked in Byron's life by a series of important beginnings and endings. In 1821 Byron began making plans, principally with Leigh Hunt and Shelley, to launch *The Liberal*. In the same year Byron's relations with his old publisher John Murray came under increasing strain because Murray found Byron's new poetical work too controversial. The break finally came in 1822, when Byron took the liberal John Hunt for his publisher.

All these events conspired to bring Byron, finally, back to his first and greatest love, Greece. In 1821, when he heard that there had been a Greek rising against Ottoman rule in the Peloponnese, Byron and Teresa's brother Pietro thought of leaving to join the struggle there. The idea remained in his mind through the early years of the Greek war of independence, but he did not finally determine to go until 1823, when he was asked to become a member of the London Greek Committee. As with the events surrounding his marriage separation, Byron's final trip to Greece would quickly assume mythic proportions in an already profoundly mythological life. There can be little doubt that Byron went to Greece either to emerge a hero from the struggle, or to die a hero in its cause. In the event, he died in a military cot in an obscure room in a small town in western Greece—of fever and the complications it induced in a body already debilitated by a life lived always at extremes and in excess. He never saw battle, and in his own mind he would have judged his last fling at heroism an utter failure.

In fact, however, his death proved useful to the revolutionary Greek forces, which often found it difficult to co-ordinate their efforts. Byron's death helped to unify the various revolutionary elements even as it also helped to consolidate European support for the Greek cause. As for Byron himself, his death seemed the crowning proof that his life had been ruled by some tremendous fate. It is a deeply, even a profoundly poetical life—not merely because it is so rich, so theatrical, and so intense, but also because it is all of a piece. His own writings, furthermore, are not merely the expressive vehicle of that mythic life; they are as well the locus of its central deeds and agencies.

V

Perhaps there are two fundamental ideals that we associate with the notion of individuality: remaining faithful, to the end, to one's essential character, and finding it possible, at some point in one's life, to begin again in a new way. To a certain extent these must be seen as contradictory, yet equally desirable, goals; yet Byron— that byword of contradictions—was able to achieve both.

Byron's greatness, in this context, lies in the fact that he lived a great individual life. It was a life lived intensely from end to end— full of pettinesses, evil, amazing and persistent follies, yet complete and thorough, like a rich and complicated poem. In the end Byron seems never to have died, which is perhaps why he continues to live as a cultural force, and always will.

William Blake proudly confessed to have 'died many times' in his life of sixty years. This is a Christian idea, to die and to be reborn to a new life (and a Protestant idea to do it over and over again). The idea of Byron's life, however, as Nietzsche was later to see so clearly, was not a Christian one. Byron was to suffer and to change, but he would not die except once, as a mortal should. To have managed this—to have always been 'Changeable too, yet somehow "idem semper"' in this way—is, I think, the central fact about Byron's cultural immortality. Shelley called him the Pilgrim of Eternity but, when Shelley's Cloud said of itself 'I change, but I cannot die', it expressed the essence of a new genealogy of morals. Blake's radical Christian mind is of another age, and we honour and submit ourselves to him because he is so unlike what we recognize and instinctively comprehend. It is otherwise with Byron, who typifies the energies and contradictions of the new European world which began to emerge in the late eighteenth century. Him we honour and study because he seems to have found a way of surviving, even triumphing over, such a world—a world which we now are beginning to suspect may be incapable of survival, at least in the spirit.

The texts of the poems in this edition are taken from the present editor's *Byron: The Complete Poetical Works* (the Oxford English Texts Edition).

Chronology

1783   Augusta Byron [Leigh] born, Byron's half-sister.

1788   Byron born, 22 January.

1789   French Revolution begins.

1793   Execution of Louis XVI; France declares war on England.

1798   Byron becomes Sixth Baron Byron; Irish Rebellion (February–October); Wordsworth's and Coleridge's *Lyrical Ballads* published.

1799   Bonaparte becomes First Consul.

1802   Peace of Amiens.

1803   England declares war on France; Byron meets and falls in love with his cousin Mary Chaworth.

1804   Napoleon made Emperor.

1805   Byron enters Trinity College, Cambridge: Nelson's victory at Trafalgar (October).

1806   *Fugitive Pieces* printed privately.

1807   *Poems on Various Occasions* and *Hours of Idleness* published: Peninsular War begins (December).

1808   *Poems Original and Translated* published; Byron takes MA degree; leaves Cambridge for Newstead Abbey.

1809   *English Bards and Scotch Reviewers* published; Byron leaves England for his trip to the Peninsula and the Levant.

1810–11 Byron in the Levant; composes first two cantos of *Childe Harold*; Prince of Wales made Regent after George III is generally acknowledged insane.

1812   Byron's maiden speech in Lords (opposing the Frame-Breaking Bill); *Childe Harold* I–II published; Napoleon's retreat from Moscow.

1813   Publication of *The Giaour* and *The Bride of Abydos*; Austria joins the Alliance against France; Southey made Poet Laureate.

1814   Publication of *The Corsair, Ode to Napoleon Buonaparte*, and *Lara*; engagement to Annabella Milbanke; invasion of France by the Allies; Napoleon exiled to Elba, the Bourbons restored; publication of Wordsworth's *Excursion* and Scott's *Waverley*.

1815   Byron's marriage, 2 January; publication of *Hebrew Melodies*;

Napoleon escapes from Elba, defeated at Waterloo; birth of Byron's daughter Ada.

1816   Lady Byron leaves Byron, 15 January; publication of *The Siege of Corinth* and *Parisina*, February; the Separation Proceedings are concluded and Byron leaves England in April for Belgium, Switzerland, and finally Italy; Byron composes and publishes *Childe Harold* III; *The Prisoner of Chillon and Other Poems* published, December; Spa Fields Riot (December).

1817   Birth of Byron's natural daughter Allegra, by Claire Clairemont, January; Byron at the Venetian Carnival; completes writing *Manfred*, published in June; Habeas Corpus suspended, March; Coleridge publishes his second *Lay Sermon* and *Biographia Literaria*; composition of *Childe Harold* IV and *Beppo*; Newstead Abbey sold, December.

1818   Habeas Corpus restored, January; Byron again at Venetian Carnival, January–February; *Beppo*, February, and *Childe Harold* IV, April, published; Keats's *Endymion* published (April); Byron leases the Palazzo Mocenigo in Venice; begins *Don Juan*, July.

1819   Venetian Carnival dissipations once again (January–February); Wordsworth publishes *Peter Bell* and *The Waggoner* (April–May); liaison with the Contessa Teresa Guiccioli begins, April; publication of *Mazeppa*, June, and *Don Juan* I–II, July; Peterloo Massacre (August) and the passage of the Six Acts (December); Byron gives his *Memoirs* to Thomas Moore, October.

1820   Death of George III, Accession of George IV (January); Cato Street Conspiracy (February); Byron increasingly involved in revolutionary activities in Italy through the Gamba family; revolution in Spain and Portugal (summer); publication of Shelley's *Prometheus Unbound* (August); trial of Queen Caroline (August–November).

1821   The Bowles Controversy (February–May); Greek Revolution begins (spring); publication of *Marino Faliero* and *The Prophecy of Dante*, April; death of Napoleon (May); the Gambas expelled from Romagna (July); *Don Juan* III–V published, August; Byron leaves to join the Shelleys and the Gambas and the Pisan Circle of friends, October; publication of *Sardanapalus*, *The Two Foscari*, and *Cain*, December.

1822   After more than a year's interruption, Byron resumes composition of *Don Juan*, January; breaks with John Murray, Byron comes to an agreement to publish with John Hunt, spring–summer; daughter Allegra dies in convent, April; Hunt joins Shelley and Byron, plans made to publish *The Liberal*, June; Shelley drowns (July); suicide of Castlereagh (August); Byron and the Hunts move to Genoa, September; *The Vision of Judgment* published in first number of *The Liberal*, October, John Hunt prosecuted for publication, December; *Werner* published, November.

1823 Publication of *Heaven and Earth*, January and *The Age of Bronze*, April; Byron's interest in the Greek Revolution ignited, he is elected a member of the London Greek Committee, April–May; publication of *The Island*, June, and *Don Juan* VI–VIII, July, IX–XI, August, XII–XIV, December; war between France and Spain (summer); Byron sails for Greece, July; agrees to lend Greek provisional government £4,000.

1824 Byron at Missolonghi; publication of *The Deformed Transformed*, February and *Don Juan* XV–XVI, April; suffers convulsions, February, health rapidly deteriorates; final illness and death, 9–19 April; burial in the Hucknall Torkard Church, Nottinghamshire.

A Fragment

When, to their airy hall, my fathers' voice,
Shall call my spirit, joyful in their choice;
When, pois'd upon the gale, my form shall ride,
Or, dark in mist, descend the mountain's side;
Oh! may my shade behold no sculptur'd urns,
To mark the spot, where earth to earth returns:
No lengthen'd scroll, no praise encumber'd stone;
My epitaph shall be, my name alone:
If *that* with honour fail to crown my clay,
Oh! may no other fame my deeds repay,   10
That, only *that*, shall single out the spot,
By that remember'd, or with that forgot.

[1806]

Damaetas

In law an infant, and in years a boy,
In mind a slave to every vicious joy,
From every sense of shame and virtue wean'd,
In lies an adept, in deceit a fiend;
Vers'd in hypocrisy, while yet a child,
Fickle as wind, of inclinations wild;
Woman his dupe, his heedless friend a tool,
Old in the world, though scarcely broke from school;
Damaetas ran through all the maze of sin,
And found the goal, when others just begin: 10
Ev'n still conflicting passions shake his soul,
And bid him drain the dregs of pleasure's bowl;
But, pall'd with vice, he breaks his former chain,
And, what was once his bliss, appears his bane.

[1807]

Written Beneath a Picture

I

Dear object of defeated care!
   Though now of Love and thee bereft,
To reconcile me with despair
   Thine image and my tears are left.

2

'Tis said with Sorrow Time can cope;
   But this I feel can ne'er be true:
For by the death-blow of my Hope
   My Memory immortal grew.

Stanzas

'Heu quanto minus est cum reliquis versari quam tui meminisse!'

I

And thou art dead, as young and fair
   As aught of mortal birth;
And form so soft, and charms so rare,
   Too soon return'd to Earth!
Though Earth receiv'd them in her bed,
And o'er the spot the crowd may tread
   In carelessness or mirth,
There is an eye which could not brook
A moment on that grave to look.

2

I will not ask where thou liest low,   10
   Nor gaze upon the spot;
There flowers or weeds at will may grow,
   So I behold them not:
It is enough for me to prove
That what I lov'd and long must love
   Like common earth can rot;

To me there needs no stone to tell
'Tis Nothing that I lov'd so well.

3

Yet did I love thee to the last
   As fervently as thou,   20
Who did'st not change through all the past,
   And can'st not alter now.
The love where Death has set his seal,
Nor age can chill, nor rival steal,
   Nor falsehood disavow:
And, what were worse, thou can'st not see
Or wrong, or change, or fault in me.

4

The better days of life were ours;
   The worst can be but mine:
The sun that cheers, the storm that lowers,   30
   Shall never more be thine.
The silence of that dreamless sleep
I envy now too much to weep;
   Nor need I to repine
That all those charms have pass'd away:
I might have watch'd through long decay.

5

The flower in ripen'd bloom unmatch'd
   Must fall the earliest prey,
Though by no hand untimately snatch'd,
   The leaves must drop away: 40
And yet it were a greater grief
To watch it withering, leaf by leaf,
   Than see it pluck'd to-day;
Since earthly eye but ill can bear
To trace the change to foul from fair.

6

   I know not if I could have borne
      To see thy beauties fade;
   The night that follow'd such a morn
      Had worn a deeper shade:

Thy day without a cloud hath past,   50
And thou wert lovely to the last;
    Extinguish'd, not decay'd;
As stars that shoot along the sky
Shine brightest as they fall from high.

7

As once I wept, if I could weep,
    My tears might well be shed,
To think I was not near to keep
    One vigil o'er thy bed;
To gaze, how fondly! on thy face,
To fold thee in a faint embrace,   60
    Uphold thy drooping head;
And show that love, however vain,
Nor thou nor I can feel again.

8

Yet how much less it were to gain,
    Though thou hast left me free,
The loveliest things that still remain,
    Than thus remember thee!
The all of thine that cannot die
Through dark and dread Eternity
    Returns again to me,   70
And more thy buried love endears
Than aught, except its living years.

[1812]

Canto II

1

Come, blue-eyed maid of heaven!—but thou, alas!
Didst never yet one mortal song inspire—
Goddess of Wisdom! here thy temple was,
And is, despite of war and wasting fire,
And years, that bade thy worship to expire:
But worse than steel, and flame, and ages slow,
Is the dread sceptre and dominion dire
Of men who never felt the sacred glow
That thoughts of thee and thine on polish'd breasts bestow.

2

Ancient of days! august Athena! where,   10
Where are thy men of might? thy grand in soul?
Gone—glimmering through the dream of things that were:
First in the race that led to Glory's goal,
They won, and pass'd away—is this the whole?
A school-boy's tale, the wonder of an hour!
The warrior's weapon and the sophist's stole
Are sought in vain, and o'er each mouldering tower,
Dim with the mist of years, grey flits the shade of power.

3

Son of the morning, rise! approach you here!
Come—but molest not yon defenceless urn: 20
Look on this spot—a nation's sepulchre!
Abode of gods, whose shrines no longer burn.
Even gods must yield—religions take their turn:
'Twas Jove's—'tis Mahomet's—and other creeds
Will rise with other years, till man shall learn
Vainly his incense soars, his victim bleeds;
Poor child of Doubt and Death, whose hope is built on reeds.

4

Bound to the earth, he lifts his eye to heaven—
Is't not enough, unhappy thing! to know
Thou art? Is this a boon so kindly given,   30
That being, thou wouldst be again, and go,
Thou know'st not, reck'st not to what region, so
On earth no more, but mingled with the skies?
Still wilt thou dream on future joy and woe?
Regard and weigh yon dust before it flies:
That little urn saith more than thousand homilies.

5

Or burst the vanish'd Hero's lofty mound;
Far on the solitary shore he sleeps:
He fell, and falling nations mourn'd around;
But now not one of saddening thousands weeps,   40
Nor warlike worshipper his vigil keeps
Where demi-gods appear'd, as records tell.
Remove yon skull from out the scatter'd heaps:
Is that a temple where a God may dwell?
Why ev'n the worm at last disdains her shatter'd cell!

6

Look on its broken arch, its ruin'd wall,
Its chambers desolate, and portals foul:
Yes, this was once Ambition's airy hall,
The dome of Thought, the palace of the Soul:
Behold through each lack-lustre, eyeless hole,   50
The gay recess of Wisdom and of Wit
And Passion's host, that never brook'd control:
Can all, saint, sage, or sophist ever writ,
People this lonely tower, this tenement refit?

7

Well didst thou speak, Athena's wisest son!
'All that we know is, nothing can be known.'
Why should we shrink from what we cannot shun?
Each has his pang, but feeble sufferers groan
With brain-born dreams of evil all their own.

Pursue what Chance or Fate proclaimeth best; 60
Peace waits us on the shores of Acheron:
There no forc'd banquet claims the sated guest,
But Silence spreads the couch of ever welcome rest.

.　　.　　.　　.　　.　　.

25

To sit on rocks, to muse o'er flood and fell,
To slowly trace the forest's shady scene,
Where things that own not man's dominion dwell,
And mortal foot hath ne'er, or rarely been;
To climb the trackless mountain all unseen,
With the wild flock that never needs a fold;
Alone o'er steeps and foaming falls to lean; 70
This is not solitude; 'tis but to hold
Converse with Nature's charms, and view her stores unroll'd.

26

But midst the crowd, the hum, the shock of men,
To hear, to see, to feel, and to possess,
And roam along, the world's tir'd denizen,
With none who bless us, none whom we can bless;
Minions of splendour shrinking from distress!
None that, with kindred consciousness endued,
If we were not, would seem to smile the less
Of all that flatter'd, follow'd, sought and sued; 80
This is to be alone; this, this is solitude!

27

More blest the life of godly Eremite,
Such as on lonely Athos may be seen,
Watching at Eve upon the giant height,
That looks o'er waves so blue, skies so serene,
That he who there at such an hour hath been
Will wistful linger on that hallow'd spot;
Then slowly tear him from the 'witching scene,
Sigh forth one wish that such had been his lot,
Then turn to hate a world he had almost forgot.
90

[1812]

THE GIAOUR

A Fragment of a Turkish Tale

One fatal remembrance—one sorrow that throws
Its bleak shade alike o'er our joys and our woes
To which Life nothing darker nor brighter can bring,
For which joy hath no balm—and affliction no sting.

MOORE

TO

SAMUEL ROGERS, ESQ.

AS A SLIGHT BUT MOST SINCERE TOKEN
OF ADMIRATION OF HIS GENIUS;
RESPECT FOR HIS CHARACTER,
AND GRATITUDE FOR HIS FRIENDSHIP;
THIS PRODUCTION IS INSCRIBED BY
HIS OBLIGED AND AFFECTIONATE SERVANT,

BYRON.

ADVERTISEMENT

The tale which these disjointed fragments present, is founded upon circumstances now less common in the East than formerly; either because the ladies are more circumspect than in the 'olden time'; or because the Christians have better fortune or less enterprise. The story, when entire, contained the adventures of a female slave, who was thrown, in the Mussulman manner, into the sea for infidelity, and avenged by a young Venetian, her lover, at the time the Seven Islands were possessed by the Republic of Venice, and soon after the Arnauts were beaten back from the Morea, which they had ravaged for some time subsequent to the Russian invasion. The desertion of the Mainotes, on being refused the plunder of Misitra, led to the abandonment of that enterprise, and to the desolation of the Morea, during which the cruelty exercised on all sides was unparalleled even in the annals of the faithful.

No breath of air to break the wave
That rolls below the Athenian's grave,
That tomb which, gleaming o'er the cliff,*
First greets the homeward-veering skiff,
High o'er the land he saved in vain—
When shall such hero live again?

　　　·　　·　　·　　·　　·　　·

　Fair clime! where every season smiles
Benignant o'er those blessed isles,
Which seen from far Colonna's height,
Make glad the heart that hails the sight,   10
And lend to loneliness delight.
There mildly dimpling—Ocean's cheek
Reflects the tints of many a peak
Caught by the laughing tides that lave
These Edens of the eastern wave;
And if at times a transient breeze
Break the blue chrystal of the seas,
Or sweep one blossom from the trees,
How welcome is each gentle air,
That wakes and wafts the odours there!   20
For there—the Rose o'er crag or vale,
Sultana of the Nightingale,*
　The maid for whom his melody—
　His thousand songs are heard on high,
Blooms blushing to her lover's tale;
His queen, the garden queen, his Rose,
Unbent by winds, unchill'd by snows,
Far from the winters of the west
By every breeze and season blest,
Returns the sweets by nature given   30
In softest incense back to heaven;
And grateful yields that smiling sky
Her fairest hue and fragrant sigh.
And many a summer flower is there,
And many a shade that love might share,
And many a grotto, meant for rest,
That holds the pirate for a guest;
Whose bark in sheltering cove below
Lurks for the passing peaceful prow,

Till the gay mariner's guitar*   40
Is heard, and seen the evening star;
Then stealing with the muffled oar,
Far shaded by the rocky shore,
Rush the night-prowlers on the prey,
And turn to groans his roundelay.
Strange—that where Nature lov'd to trace,
As if for Gods, a dwelling-place,
And every charm and grace hath mixed
Within the paradise she fixed—
There man, enamour'd of distress,   50
Should mar it into wilderness,
And trample, brute-like, o'er each flower
That tasks not one laborious hour;
Nor claims the culture of his hand
To bloom along the fairy land,
But springs as to preclude his care,
And sweetly woos him—but to spare!
Strange—that where all is peace beside
There passion riots in her pride,
And lust and rapine wildly reign,   60
To darken o'er the fair domain.
It is as though the fiends prevail'd
Against the seraphs they assail'd,
And fixed, on heavenly thrones, should dwell
The freed inheritors of hell—
So soft the scene, so form'd for joy,
So curst the tyrants that destroy!

    He who hath bent him o'er the dead,
Ere the first day of death is fled;
The first dark day of nothingness,   70
The last of danger and distress;
(Before Decay's effacing fingers
Have swept the lines where beauty lingers)
And mark'd the mild angelic air—
The rapture of repose that's there—
The fixed yet tender traits that streak
The languor of the placid cheek,
And—but for that sad shrouded eye,

That fires not—wins not—weeps not—now—
And but for that chill changeless brow,   80
Where cold Obstruction's apathy*
Appals the gazing mourner's heart,
As if to him it could impart
The doom he dreads, yet dwells upon—
Yes—but for these and these alone,
Some moments—aye—one treacherous hour,
He still might doubt the tyrant's power,
So fair—so calm—so softly seal'd
The first—last look—by death reveal'd!*
Such is the aspect of this shore—   90
'Tis Greece—but living Greece no more!
So coldly sweet, so deadly fair,
We start—for soul is wanting there.
Hers is the loveliness in death,
That parts not quite with parting breath;
But beauty with that fearful bloom,
That hue which haunts it to the tomb—
Expression's last receding ray,
A gilded halo hovering round decay,
The farewell beam of Feeling past away!   100
Spark of that flame—perchance of heavenly birth—
Which gleams—but warms no more its cherish'd
      earth!

Clime of the unforgotten brave!—
Whose land from plain to mountain-cave
Was Freedom's home or Glory's grave—
Shrine of the mighty! can it be,
That this is all remains of thee?
Approach thou craven crouching slave—
Say, is not this Thermopylae?
These waters blue that round you lave   110
Oh servile offspring of the free—
Pronounce what sea, what shore is this?
The gulf, the rock of Salamis!
These scenes—their story not unknown—
Arise, and make again your own;
Snatch from the ashes of your sires
The embers of their former fires,

And he who in the strife expires
Will add to theirs a name of fear,
That Tyranny shall quake to hear,   120
And leave his sons a hope, a fame,
They too will rather die than shame;
For Freedom's battle once begun,
Bequeathed by bleeding Sire to Son,
Though baffled oft is ever won.
Bear witness, Greece, thy living page,
Attest it many a deathless age!
While kings in dusty darkness hid,
Have left a nameless pyramid,
Thy heroes—though the general doom   130
Hath swept the column from their tomb,
A mightier monument command,
The mountains of their native land!
There points thy Muse to stranger's eye,
The graves of those that cannot die!
'Twere long to tell, and sad to trace,
Each step from splendour to disgrace,
Enough—no foreign foe could quell
Thy soul, till from itself it fell,
Yes! Self-abasement pav'd the way   140
To villain-bonds and despot-sway.

What can he tell who treads thy shore?
   No legend of thine olden time,
No theme on which the muse might soar,
High as thine own in days of yore,
   When man was worthy of thy clime.
The hearts within thy valleys bred,
The fiery souls that might have led
   Thy sons to deeds sublime;
Now crawl from cradle to the grave,   150
Slaves—nay, the bondsmen of a slave,*
   And callous, save to crime;
Stain'd with each evil that pollutes
Mankind, where least above the brutes;
Without even savage virtue blest,
Without one free or valiant breast.
Still to the neighbouring ports they waft

Proverbial wiles, and ancient craft,
In this the subtle Greek is found,
For this, and this alone, renown'd.   160
In vain might Liberty invoke
The spirit to its bondage broke,
Or raise the neck that courts the yoke:
No more her sorrows I bewail,
Yet this will be a mournful tale,
And they who listen may believe,
Who heard it first had cause to grieve.

. . . . .

Far, dark, along the blue sea glancing,
The shadows of the rocks advancing,
Start on the fisher's eye like boat   170
Of island-pirate or Mainote;
And fearful for his light caique
He shuns the near but doubtful creek,
Though worn and weary with his toil,
And cumber'd with his scaly spoil,
Slowly, yet strongly, plies the oar,
Till Port Leone's safer shore
Receives him by the lovely light
That best becomes an Eastern night.

. . . . .

Who thundering comes on blackest steed?   180
With slacken'd bit and hoof of speed,
Beneath the chattering iron's sound
The cavern'd echoes wake around
In lash for lash, and bound for bound;
The foam that streaks the courser's side,
Seems gather'd from the ocean-tide:
Though weary waves are sunk to rest,
There's none within his rider's breast,
And though to-morrow's tempest lower,
'Tis calmer than thy heart, young Giaour!*   190
I know thee not, I loathe thy race,
But in thy lineaments I trace
What time shall strengthen, not efface;

Though young and pale, that sallow front
Is scath'd by fiery passion's brunt,
Though bent on earth thine evil eye
As meteor-like thou glidest by,
Right well I view, and deem thee one
Whom Othman's sons should slay or shun.

   On—on he hastened—and he drew   200
My gaze of wonder as he flew:
Though like a demon of the night
He passed and vanished from my sight;
His aspect and his air impressed
A troubled memory on my breast;
And long upon my startled ear
Rung his dark courser's hoofs of fear.
He spurs his steed—he nears the steep,
That jutting shadows o'er the deep—
He winds around—he hurries by—   210
The rock relieves him from mine eye—
For well I ween unwelcome he
Whose glance is fixed on those that flee;
And not a star but shines too bright
On him who takes such timeless flight.
He wound along—but ere he passed
One glance he snatched—as if his last—
A moment checked his wheeling steed—
A moment breathed him from his speed—
A moment on his stirrup stood—   220
Why looks he o'er the olive wood?—
The crescent glimmers on the hill,
The Mosque's high lamps are quivering still;
Though too remote for sound to wake
In echoes of the far tophaike,*
The flashes of each joyous peal
Are seen to prove the Moslem's zeal.
To-night—set Rhamazani's sun—
To-night—the Bairam feast's begun—
To-night—but who and what art thou   230
Of foreign garb and fearful brow?
And what are these to thine or thee,
That thou should'st either pause or flee?

He stood—some dread was on his face—
Soon Hatred settled in its place—
It rose not with the reddening flush
Of transient Anger's hasty blush,
But pale as marble o'er the tomb,
Whose ghastly whiteness aids its gloom.
His brow was bent—his eye was glazed—   240
He raised his arm, and fiercely raised;
And sternly shook his hand on high,
As doubting to return or fly;—
Impatient of his flight delayed
Here loud his raven charger neighed—
Down glanced that hand, and grasped his blade—
That sound had burst his waking dream,
As Slumber starts at owlet's scream.—
The spur hath lanced his courser's sides—
Away—away—for life he rides—   250
Swift as the hurled on high jerreed,*
Springs to the touch his startled steed,
The rock is doubled—and the shore
Shakes with the clattering tramp no more—
The crag is won—no more is seen
His Christian crest and haughty mien.—
'Twas but an instant—he restrained
That fiery barb so sternly reined—
'Twas but a moment that he stood,
Then sped as if by death pursued;   260
But in that instant, o'er his soul
Winters of Memory seemed to roll,
And gather in that drop of time
A life of pain, an age of crime.
O'er him who loves, or hates, or fears,
Such moment pours the grief of years—
What felt *he* then—at once opprest
By all that most distracts the breast?
That pause—which pondered o'er his fate,
Oh, who its dreary length shall date!   270
Though in Time's record nearly nought,
It was Eternity to Thought!
For infinite as boundless space
The thought that Conscience must embrace,

Which in itself can comprehend
Woe without name—or hope—or end.—

    The hour is past, the Giaour is gone,
And did he fly or fall alone?
Woe to that hour he came or went,
The curse for Hassan's sin was sent   280
To turn a palace to a tomb;
He came, he went, like the Simoom,*
That harbinger of fate and gloom,
Beneath whose widely-wasting breath
The very cypress droops to death—
Dark tree—still sad, when others' grief is fled,
The only constant mourner o'er the dead!

    The steed is vanished from the stall,
No serf is seen in Hassan's hall;
The lonely Spider's thin grey pall   290
Waves slowly widening o'er the wall;
The Bat builds in his Haram bower;
And in the fortress of his power
The Owl usurps the beacon-tower;
The wild-dog howls o'er the fountain's brim,
With baffled thirst, and famine, grim,
For the stream has shrunk from its marble bed,
Where the weeds and the desolate dust are spread.
'Twas sweet of yore to see it play
And chase the sultriness of day—   300
As springing high the silver dew
In whirls fantastically flew,
And flung luxurious coolness round
The air, and verdure o'er the ground.—
'Twas sweet, when cloudless stars were bright,
To view the wave of watery light,
And hear its melody by night.—
And oft had Hassan's Childhood played
Around the verge of that cascade;
And oft upon his mother's breast   310
That sound had harmonized his rest;
And oft had Hassan's Youth along
Its bank been sooth'd by Beauty's song;

And softer seemed each melting tone
Of Music mingled with its own.—
But ne'er shall Hassan's Age repose
Along the brink at Twilight's close—
The stream that filled that font is fled—
The blood that warmed his heart is shed!—
And here no more shall human voice   320
Be heard to rage—regret—rejoice—
The last sad note that swelled the gale
Was woman's wildest funeral wail—
That quenched in silence—all is still,
But the lattice that flaps when the wind is shrill—
Though raves the gust, and floods the rain,
No hand shall close its clasp again.
On desert sands 'twere joy to scan
The rudest steps of fellow man,
So here the very voice of Grief   330
Might wake an Echo like relief—
At least 'twould say, 'all are not gone;
There lingers Life, though but in one'—
For many a gilded chamber's there,
Which Solitude might well forbear;
Within that dome as yet Decay
Hath slowly worked her cankering way—
But Gloom is gathered o'er the gate,
Nor there the Fakir's self will wait;
Nor there will wandering Dervise stay,   340
For Bounty cheers not his delay;
Nor there will weary stranger halt
To bless the sacred 'bread and salt'.*
Alike must Wealth and Poverty
Pass heedless and unheeded by,
For Courtesy and Pity died
With Hassan on the mountain side.—
His roof—that refuge unto men—
Is Desolation's hungry den.—
The guest flies the hall, and the vassal from labour, 350
Since his turban was cleft by the infidel's sabre!*

.   .   .   .

I hear the sound of coming feet,
But not a voice mine ear to greet—
More near—each turban I can scan,
And silver-sheathed ataghan;*
The foremost of the band is seen
An Emir by his garb of green:*
  'Ho! who art thou!'—'this low salam*
  Replies of Moslem faith I am.'
'The burthen ye so gently bear,   360
Seems one that claims your utmost care,
And, doubtless, holds some precious freight,
My humble bark would gladly wait.'

  'Thou speakest sooth, thy skiff unmoor,
And waft us from the silent shore;
Nay, leave the sail still furl'd, and ply
The nearest oar that's scatter'd by,
And midway to those rocks where sleep
The channel'd waters dark and deep.—
Rest from your task—so—bravely done,   370
Our course has been right swiftly run,
Yet 'tis the longest voyage, I trow,
That one of'—   .   .   .   .

     .   .   .   .   .

  Sullen it plunged, and slowly sank,
The calm wave rippled to the bank;
I watch'd it as it sank, methought
Some motion from the current caught
Bestirr'd it more,—'twas but the beam
That chequer'd o'er the living stream—
I gaz'd, till vanishing from view,   380
Like lessening pebble it withdrew;
Still less and less, a speck of white
That gemm'd the tide, then mock'd the sight;
And all its hidden secrets sleep,
Known but to Genii of the deep,
Which, trembling in their coral caves,
They dare not whisper to the waves.

     .   .   .   .   .

As rising on its purple wing
The insect-queen of eastern spring,*
O'er emerald meadows of Kashmeer   390
Invites the young pursuer near,
And leads him on from flower to flower
A weary chase and wasted hour,
Then leaves him, as it soars on high
With panting heart and tearful eye:
So Beauty lures the full-grown child
With hue as bright, and wing as wild;
A chase of idle hopes and fears,
Begun in folly, closed in tears.
If won, to equal ills betrayed,   400
Woe waits the insect and the maid,
A life of pain, the loss of peace,
From infant's play, or man's caprice:
The lovely toy so fiercely sought
Has lost its charm by being caught,
For every touch that wooed its stay
Has brush'd the brightest hues away
Till charm, and hue, and beauty gone,
'Tis left to fly or fall alone.
With wounded wing, or bleeding breast,   410
Ah! where shall either victim rest?
Can this with faded pinion soar
From rose to tulip as before?
Or Beauty, blighted in an hour,
Find joy within her broken bower?
No: gayer insects fluttering by
Ne'er droop the wing o'er those that die,
And lovelier things have mercy shewn
To every failing but their own,
And every woe a tear can claim   420
Except an erring sister's shame.

   .   .   .   .   .   .

The Mind, that broods o'er guilty woes,
  Is like the Scorpion girt by fire,
In circle narrowing as it glows
The flames around their captive close,

Till inly search'd by thousand throes,
　　And maddening in her ire,
One sad and sole relief she knows,
The sting she nourish'd for her foes,
Whose venom never yet was vain,   430
Gives but one pang, and cures all pain,
And darts into her desperate brain.—
So do the dark in soul expire,
Or live like Scorpion girt by fire;*
So writhes the mind Remorse hath riven,
Unfit for earth, undoom'd for heaven,
Darkness above, despair beneath,
Around it flame, within it death!—

　　　　　.　　　.　　　.　　　.　　　.　　　.

　　Black Hassan from the Haram flies,
Nor bends on woman's form his eyes,   440
The unwonted chase each hour employs,
Yet shares he not the hunter's joys.
Not thus was Hassan wont to fly
When Leila dwelt in his Serai.
Doth Leila there no longer dwell?
That tale can only Hassan tell:
Strange rumours in our city say
Upon that eve she fled away;
When Rhamazan's last sun was set,*
And flashing from each minaret   450
Millions of lamps proclaim'd the feast
Of Bairam through the boundless East.
'Twas then she went as to the bath,
Which Hassan vainly search'd in wrath,
But she was flown her master's rage
In likeness of a Georgian page;
And far beyond the Moslem's power
Had wrong'd him with the faithless Giaour.
Somewhat of this had Hassan deem'd,
But still so fond, so fair she seem'd,   460
Too well he trusted to the slave
Whose treachery deserv'd a grave:
And on that eve had gone to mosque,

And thence to feast in his kiosk.
Such is the tale his Nubians tell,
Who did not watch their charge too well;
But others say, that on that night,
By pale Phingari's trembling light,*
The Giaour upon his jet-black steed
Was seen—but seen alone to speed   470
With bloody spur along the shore,
Nor maid nor page behind him bore.

. . . . . .

Her eye's dark charm 'twere vain to tell,
But gaze on that of the Gazelle,
It will assist thy fancy well,
As large, as languishingly dark,
But Soul beam'd forth in every spark
That darted from beneath the lid,
Bright as the jewel of Giamschid.*
Yea, *Soul*, and should our prophet say   480
That form was nought but breathing clay,
By Alla! I would answer nay;
Though on Al-Sirat's arch I stood,*
Which totters o'er the fiery flood,
With Paradise within my view,
And all his Houris beckoning through.
Oh! who young Leila's glance could read
And keep that portion of his creed*
Which saith, that woman is but dust,
A soulless toy for tyrant's lust?   490
On her might Muftis gaze, and own
That through her eye the Immortal shone—
On her fair cheek's unfading hue,
The young pomegranate's blossoms strew*
Their bloom in blushes ever new—
Her hair in hyacinthine flow*
When left to roll its folds below,
As midst her handmaids in the hall
She stood superior to them all,
Hath swept the marble where her feet   500
Gleamed whiter than the mountain sleet

Ere from the cloud that gave it birth,
It fell, and caught one stain of earth.
The cygnet nobly walks the water—
So moved on earth Circassia's daughter—
The loveliest bird of Franguestan!*
As rears her crest the ruffled Swan,
   And spurns the wave with wings of pride,
When pass the steps of stranger man
   Along the banks that bound her tide;   510
Thus rose fair Leila's whiter neck:—
Thus armed with beauty would she check
Intrusion's glance, till Folly's gaze
Shrunk from the charms it meant to praise.
Thus high and graceful was her gait;
Her heart as tender to her mate—
Her mate—stern Hassan, who was he?
Alas! that name was not for thee!

.   .   .   .   .   .

   Stern Hassan hath a journey ta'en
With twenty vassals in his train,   520
Each arm'd as best becomes a man
With arquebuss and ataghan;
The chief before, as deck'd for war,
Bears in his belt the scimitar
Stain'd with the best of Arnaut blood,
When in the pass the rebels stood,
And few return'd to tell the tale
Of what befell in Parne's vale.
The pistols which his girdle bore
Were those that once a pasha wore,   530
Which still, though gemm'd and boss'd with
   gold,
Even robbers tremble to behold.—
'Tis said he goes to woo a bride
More true than her who left his side;
The faithless slave that broke her bower,
And, worse than faithless, for a Giaour!—

.   .   .   .   .   .

The sun's last rays are on the hill,
And sparkle in the fountain rill,
Whose welcome waters cool and clear,
Draw blessings from the mountaineer;   540
Here may the loitering merchant Greek
Find that repose 'twere vain to seek
In cities lodg'd too near his lord,
And trembling for his secret hoard—
Here may he rest where none can see,
In crowds a slave, in desarts free;
And with forbidden wine may stain
The bowl a Moslem must not drain.—

    .   .   .   .   .

The foremost Tartar's in the gap,
Conspicuous by his yellow cap,   550
The rest in lengthening line the while
Wind slowly through the long defile;
Above, the mountain rears a peak,
Where vultures whet the thirsty beak,
And theirs may be a feast to-night,
Shall tempt them down ere morrow's light.
Beneath, a river's wintry stream
Has shrunk before the summer beam,
And left a channel bleak and bare,
Save shrubs that spring to perish there.   560
Each side the midway path there lay
Small broken crags of granite gray,
By time or mountain lightning riven,
From summits clad in mists of heaven;
For where is he that hath beheld
The peak of Liakura unveil'd?

    .   .   .   .   .

They reach the grove of pine at last,
'Bismillah! now the peril's past;*
For yonder view the opening plain,
And there we'll prick our steeds amain':   570
The Chiaus spake, and as he said,
A bullet whistled o'er his head;

The foremost Tartar bites the ground!
　　Scarce had they time to check the rein
Swift from their steeds the riders bound,
　　But three shall never mount again;
Unseen the foes that gave the wound,
　　The dying ask revenge in vain.
With steel unsheath'd, and carbine bent,
Some o'er their courser's harness leant,　　　　　580
　　Half shelter'd by the steed,
Some fly behind the nearest rock,
And there await the coming shock,
　　Nor tamely stand to bleed
Beneath the shaft of foes unseen,
Who dare not quit their craggy screen.
Stern Hassan only from his horse
Disdains to light, and keeps his course,
Till fiery flashes in the van
Proclaim too sure the robber-clan　　　　　　590
Have well secur'd the only way
Could now avail the promis'd prey;
Then curl'd his very beard with ire,*
And glared his eye with fiercer fire.
'Though far and near the bullets hiss,
I've scaped a bloodier hour than this.'
And now the foe their covert quit,
And call his vassals to submit;
But Hassan's frown and furious word
Are dreaded more than hostile sword,　　　　　600
Nor of his little band a man
Resign'd carbine or ataghan—
Nor raised the craven cry, Amaun!*
In fuller sight, more near and near,
The lately ambush'd foes appear,
And issuing from the grove advance,
Some who on battle charger prance.—
Who leads them on with foreign brand,
Far flashing in his red right hand?
' 'Tis he—'tis he—I know him now,　　　　　610
I know him by his pallid brow;
I know him by the evil eye*
That aids his envious treachery;

I know him by his jet-black barb,
Though now array'd in Arnaut garb,
Apostate from his own vile faith,
It shall not save him from the death;
'Tis he, well met in any hour,
Lost Leila's love—accursed Giaour!'

    As rolls the river into ocean,   620
In sable torrent wildly streaming;
    As the sea-tide's opposing motion
In azure column proudly gleaming,
Beats back the current many a rood,
In curling foam and mingling flood;
While eddying whirl, and breaking wave,
Roused by the blast of winter rave;
Through sparkling spray in thundering clash,
The lightnings of the waters flash
In awful whiteness o'er the shore,   630
That shines and shakes beneath the roar;
Thus—as the stream and ocean greet,
With waves that madden as they meet—
Thus join the bands whom mutual wrong,
And fate and fury drive along.
The bickering sabres' shivering jar;
    And pealing wide—or ringing near,
    Its echoes on the throbbing ear,
The deathshot hissing from afar—
The shock—the shout—the groan of war—   640
    Reverberate along that vale,
    More suited to the shepherd's tale:
Though few the numbers—theirs the strife,
That neither spares nor speaks for life!
Ah! fondly youthful hearts can press,
To seize and share the dear caress;
But Love itself could never pant
For all that Beauty sighs to grant,
With half the fervour Hate bestows
Upon the last embrace of foes,   650
When grappling in the fight they fold
Those arms that ne'er shall lose their hold;
Friends meet to part–Love laughs at faith;—

True foes, once met, are joined till death!

     .   .   .   .

With sabre shiver'd to the hilt,
Yet dripping with the blood he spilt;
Yet strain'd within the sever'd hand
Which quivers round that faithless brand;
His turban far behind him roll'd,
And cleft in twain its firmest fold;   660
His flowing robe by falchion torn,
And crimson as those clouds of morn
That streak'd with dusky red, portend
The day shall have a stormy end;
A stain on every bush that bore
A fragment of his palampore,*
His breast with wounds unnumber'd riven,
His back to earth, his face to heaven,
Fall'n Hassan lies—his unclos'd eye
Yet lowering on his enemy,   670
As if the hour that seal'd his fate,
Surviving left his quenchless hate;
And o'er him bends that foe with brow
As dark as this that bled below.—

     .   .   .   .

  'Yes, Leila sleeps beneath the wave,
But his shall be a redder grave;
Her spirit pointed well the steel
Which taught that felon heart to feel.
He call'd the Prophet, but his power
Was vain against the vengeful Giaour: 680
He call'd on Alla—but the word
Arose unheeded or unheard.
Thou Paynim fool!—could Leila's prayer
Be pass'd, and thine accorded there?
I watch'd my time, I leagu'd with these,
The traitor in his turn to seize;
My wrath is wreak'd, the deed is done,
And now I go—but go alone.'

     .   .   .   .

     .   .   .   .

The browzing camels' bells are tinkling—
His Mother looked from her lattice high,   690
   She saw the dews of eve besprinkling
The pasture green beneath her eye,
   She saw the planets faintly twinkling,
' 'Tis twilight—sure his train is nigh.'—
She could not rest in the garden-bower,
But gazed through the grate of his steepest tower—
'Why comes he not? his steeds are fleet,
Nor shrink they from the summer heat;
Why sends not the Bridegroom his promised gift,
Is his heart more cold, or his barb less swift?   700
Oh, false reproach! yon Tartar now
Has gained our nearest mountain's brow,
And warily the steep descends,
And now within the valley bends;
And he bears the gift at his saddle bow—
How could I deem his courser slow?
Right well my largess shall repay
His welcome speed, and weary way.'—
The Tartar lighted at the gate,
But scarce upheld his fainting weight;   710
His swarthy visage spake distress,
But this might be from weariness;
His garb with sanguine spots was dyed,
But these might be from his courser's side;—
He drew the token from his vest—
Angel of Death! 'tis Hassan's cloven crest!
His calpac rent—his caftan red—*
'Lady, a fearful bride thy Son hath wed—
Me, not from mercy, did they spare,
But this empurpled pledge to bear.   720
Peace to the brave! whose blood is spilt—
Woe to the Giaour! for his the guilt.'

    .   .   .   .

   A turban carv'd in coarsest stone,*
A pillar with rank weeds o'ergrown,
Wheron can now be scarcely read
The Koran verse that mourns the dead;

Point out the spot where Hassan fell
A victim in that lonely dell.
There sleeps as true an Osmanlie
As e'er at Mecca bent the knee;   730
As ever scorn'd forbidden wine,
Or pray'd with face towards the shrine,
In orisons resumed anew
At solemn sound of 'Alla Hu!'*
Yet died he by a stranger's hand,
And stranger in his native land—
Yet died he as in arms he stood,
And unaveng'd, at least in blood.
But him the maids of Paradise
    Impatient to their halls invite,   740
And the dark Heaven of Houri's eyes
    On him shall glance for ever bright;
They come—their kerchiefs green they wave,*
And welcome with a kiss the brave!
Who falls in battle 'gainst a Giaour,
Is worthiest an immortal bower.

              .   .   .   .   .   .

    But thou, false Infidel! shalt writhe
Beneath avenging Monkir's scythe;*
And from its torment 'scape alone
To wander round lost Eblis' throne;*   750
And fire unquench'd, unquenchable—
Around—within—thy heart shall dwell,
Nor ear can hear, nor tongue can tell
The tortures of that inward hell!—
But first, on earth as Vampire sent,*
Thy corse shall from its tomb be rent;
Then ghastly haunt thy native place,
And suck the blood of all thy race,
There from thy daughter, sister, wife,
At midnight drain the stream of life;   760
Yet loathe the banquet which perforce
Must feed thy livid living corse;
Thy victims ere they yet expire
Shall know the daemon for their sire,

As cursing thee, thou cursing them,
Thy flowers are wither'd on the stem.
But one that for thy crime must fall—
The youngest—most belov'd of all,
Shall bless thee with a *father*'s name—
That word shall wrap thy heart in flame!   770
Yet must thou end thy task, and mark
Her cheek's last tinge, her eye's last spark,
And the last glassy glance must view
Which freezes o'er its lifeless blue;
Then with unhallowed hand shalt tear
The tresses of her yellow hair,
Of which in life a lock when shorn,
Affection's fondest pledge was worn;
But now is borne away by thee,
Memorial of thine agony!   780
Wet with thine own best blood shall drip,*
Thy gnashing tooth and haggard lip;
Then stalking to thy sullen grave—
Go—and with Gouls and Afrits rave;
Till these in horror shrink away
From spectre more accursed than they!

.   .   .   .   .   .

'How name ye yon lone Caloyer?
   His features I have scann'd before
In mine own land—'tis many a year,
   Since, dashing by the lonely shore,   790
I saw him urge as fleet a steed
As ever serv'd a horseman's need.
But once I saw that face—yet then
It was so mark'd with inward pain
I could not pass it by again;
It breathes the same dark spirit now,
As death were stamped upon his brow.'

' 'Tis twice three years at summer tide
   Since first among our freres he came;
And here it soothes him to abide   800
   For some dark deed he will not name.

But never at our vesper prayer,
Nor e'er before confession chair
Kneels he, nor recks he when arise
Incense or anthem to the skies,
But broods within his cell alone,
His faith and race alike unknown.
The sea from Paynim land he crost,
And here ascended from the coast,
Yet seems he not of Othman race,   810
But only Christian in his face:
I'd judge him some stray renegade,
Repentant of the change he made,
Save that he shuns our holy shrine,
Nor tastes the sacred bread and wine.
Great largess to these walls he brought,
And thus our abbot's favour bought;
But were I Prior, not a day
Should brook such stranger's further stay,
Or pent within our penance cell   820
Should doom him there for aye to dwell.
Much in his visions mutters he
Of maiden 'whelmed beneath the sea;
Of sabres clashing—foemen flying,
Wrongs aveng'd—and Moslem dying.
On cliff he hath been known to stand,
And rave as to some bloody hand
Fresh sever'd from its parent limb,
Invisible to all but him,
Which beckons onward to his grave,   830
And lures to leap into the wave.'

              .   .   .   .   .

              .   .   .   .   .

Dark and unearthly is the scowl
That glares beneath his dusky cowl—
The flash of that dilating eye
Reveals too much of times gone by—
Though varying—indistinct its hue,
Oft will his glance the gazer rue—

For in it lurks that nameless spell
Which speaks—itself unspeakable—
A spirit yet unquelled and high   840
That claims and keeps ascendancy,
And like the bird whose pinions quake—
But cannot fly the gazing snake—
Will others quail beneath his look,
Nor 'scape the glance they scarce can brook.
From him the half-affrighted Friar
When met alone would fain retire—
As if that eye and bitter smile
Transferred to others fear and guile—
Not oft to smile descendeth he,   850
And when he doth 'tis sad to see
That he but mocks at Misery.
How that pale lip will curl and quiver!
Then fix once more as if for ever—
As if his sorrow or disdain
Forbade him e'er to smile again.—
Well were it so—such ghastly mirth
From joyaunce ne'er deriv'd its birth.—
But sadder still it were to trace
What once were feelings in that face—   860
Time hath not yet the features fixed,
But brighter traits with evil mixed—
And there are hues not always faded,
Which speak a mind not all degraded
Even by the crimes through which it waded—
The common crowd but see the gloom
Of wayward deeds—and fitting doom—
The close observer can espy
A noble soul, and lineage high.—
Alas! though both bestowed in vain,   870
Which Grief could change—and Guilt could stain—
It was no vulgar tenement
To which such lofty gifts were lent,
And still with little less than dread
    On such the sight is riveted.—
The roofless cot decayed and rent,
    Will scarce delay the passer by—
The tower by war or tempest bent,

While yet may frown one battlement,
   Demands and daunts the stranger's eye—   880
Each ivied arch—and pillar lone,
Pleads haughtily for glories gone!
'His floating robe around him folding,
   Slow sweeps he through the columned aisle—
With dread beheld—with gloom beholding
   The rites that sanctify the pile.
But when the anthem shakes the choir,
And kneel the monks—his steps retire—
By yonder lone and wavering torch
His aspect glares within the porch;   890
There will he pause till all is done—
And hear the prayer—but utter none.
See—by the half-illumin'd wall
His hood fly back—his dark hair fall—
That pale brow wildly wreathing round,
As if the Gorgon there had bound
The sablest of the serpent-braid
That o'er her fearful forehead strayed.
For he declines the convent oath,
And leaves those locks' unhallowed growth—   900
But wears our garb in all beside;
And—not from piety but pride
Gives wealth to walls that never heard
Of his one holy vow nor word.—
Lo!—mark ye—as the harmony
Peals louder praises to the sky—
That livid cheek—that stoney air
Of mixed defiance and despair!
Saint Francis! keep him from the shrine!
Else may we dread the wrath divine   910
Made manifest by awful sign.—
If ever evil angel bore
The form of mortal, such he wore—
By all my hope of sins forgiven
Such looks are not of earth nor heaven!'

To love the softest hearts are prone,
But such can ne'er be all his own;
Too timid in his woes to share,

Too meek to meet, or brave, despair;
And sterner hearts alone may feel   920
The wound that time can never heal.
The rugged metal of the mine
Must burn before its surface shine,
But plung'd within the furnace-flame,
It bends and melts—though still the same;
Then tempered to thy want, or will,
'Twill serve thee to defend or kill;
A breast-plate for thine hour of need,
Or blade to bid thy foeman bleed;
But if a dagger's form it bear,   930
Let those who shape its edge, beware!
Thus passion's fire, and woman's art,
Can turn and tame the sterner heart;
From these its form and tone are ta'en,
And what they make it, must remain,
But break—before it bend again.

.   .   .   .   .   .

.   .   .   .   .   .

If solitude succeed to grief,
Release from pain is slight relief;
The vacant bosom's wilderness
Might thank the pang that made it less.   940
We loathe what none are left to share—
Even bliss—'twere woe alone to bear;
The heart once left thus desolate,
Must fly at last for ease—to hate.
It is as if the dead could feel
The icy worm around them steal;
And shudder, as the reptiles creep
To revel o'er their rotting sleep
Without the power to scare away
The cold consumers of their clay!   950
It is as if the desart-bird,*
    Whose beak unlocks her bosom's stream
    To still her famish'd nestlings' scream,
Nor mourns a life to them transferr'd,
Should rend her rash devoted breast,

And find them flown her empty nest.
The keenest pangs the wretched find
   Are rapture to the dreary void—
The leafless desart of the mind—
   The waste of feelings unemploy'd—   960
Who would be doom'd to gaze upon
A sky without a cloud or sun?
Less hideous far the tempest's roar,
Than ne'er to brave the billows more—
Thrown, when the war of winds is o'er,
A lonely wreck on fortune's shore,
'Mid sullen calm, and silent bay,
Unseen to drop by dull decay;—
Better to sink beneath the shock
That moulder piecemeal on the rock!   970

     .   .   .   .   .   .

'Father! thy days have pass'd in peace,
   'Mid counted beads, and countless prayer;
To bid the sins of others cease,
   Thyself without a crime or care,
Save transient ills that all must bear,
Has been thy lot, from youth to age,
And thou wilt bless thee from the rage
Of passions fierce and uncontroll'd,
Such as thy penitents unfold,
Whose secret sins and sorrows rest   980
Within thy pure and pitying breast.
My days, though few, have pass'd below
In much of joy, but more of woe;
Yet still in hours of love or strife,
I've 'scap'd the weariness of life;
Now leagu'd with friends, now girt by foes,
I loath'd the languor of repose;
Now nothing left to love or hate,
No more with hope or pride elate;
I'd rather be the thing that crawls   990
Most noxious o'er a dungeon's walls,
Than pass my dull, unvarying days,
Condemn'd to meditate and gaze—

Yet, lurks a wish within my breast
For rest—but not to feel 'tis rest—
Soon shall my fate that wish fulfil;
   And I shall sleep without the dream
Of what I was, and would be still;
   Dark as to thee my deeds may seem—
My memory now is but the tomb   1000
Of joys long dead—my hope—their doom—
Though better to have died with those
Than bear a life of lingering woes—
My spirit shrunk not to sustain
The searching throes of ceaseless pain;
Nor sought the self-accorded grave
Of ancient fool, and modern knave:
Yet death I have not fear'd to meet,
And in the field it had been sweet
Had danger wooed me on to move   1010
The slave of glory, not of love.
I've brav'd it—not for honour's boast;
I smile at laurels won or lost.—
To such let others carve their way,
For high renown, or hireling pay;
But place again before my eyes
Aught that I deem a worthy prize;—
The maid I love—the man I hate—
And I will hunt the steps of fate,
(To save or slay—as these require)   1020
Through rending steel, and rolling fire;
Nor need'st thou doubt this speech from one
Who would but do—what he *hath* done.
Death is but what the haughty brave—
The weak must bear—the wretch must crave—
Then let Life go to him who gave:
I have not quailed to danger's brow—
When high and happy—need I *now*?

   .   .   .   .   .

'I lov'd her, friar! nay, adored—
   But these are words that all can use—   1030
I prov'd it more in deed than word—

There's blood upon that dinted sword—
  A stain its steel can never lose:
'Twas shed for her, who died for me,
  It warmed the heart of one abhorred:
Nay, start not—no—nor bend thy knee,
  Nor midst my sins such act record,
Thou wilt absolve me from the deed,
For he was hostile to thy creed!
The very name of Nazarene   1040
Was wormwood to his Paynim spleen,
Ungrateful fool! since but for brands,
Well wielded in some hardy hands;
And wounds by Galileans given,
The surest pass to Turkish heav'n;
For him his Houris still might wait
Impatient at the prophet's gate.
I lov'd her—love will find its way
Through paths where wolves would fear to prey,
And if it dares enough, 'twere hard   1050
If passion met not some reward—
No matter how—or where—or why,
I did not vainly seek—nor sigh:
Yet sometimes with remorse in vain
I wish she had not lov'd again.
She died—I dare not tell thee how,
But look—'tis written on my brow!
There read of Cain the curse and crime,
In characters unworn by time:
Still, ere thou dost condemn me—pause—   1060
Not mine the act, though I the cause;
Yet did he but what I had done
Had she been false to more than one;
Faithless to him—he gave the blow,
But true to me—I laid him low;
Howe'er deserv'd her doom might be,
Her treachery was truth to me;
To me she gave her heart, that all
Which tyranny can ne'er enthrall;
And I, alas! too late to save,   1070
Yet all I then could give—I gave—
'Twas some relief—our foe a grave.

His death sits lightly; but her fate
Has made me—what thou well may'st hate.
His doom was seal'd—he knew it well,
    Warn'd by the voice of stern Taheer,
    Deep in whose darkly boding ear*
    The deathshot peal'd of murder near—
As filed the troop to where they fell!
    He died too in the battle broil—   1080
    A time that heeds nor pain nor toil—
    One cry to Mahomet for aid,
    One prayer to Alla—all he made:
He knew and crossed me in the fray—
I gazed upon him where he lay,
And watched his spirit ebb away;
Though pierced like Pard by hunters' steel,
He felt not half that now I feel.
I search'd, but vainly search'd to find,
The workings of a wounded mind;   1090
Each feature of that sullen corse
Betrayed his rage, but no remorse.
Oh, what had Vengeance given to trace
Despair upon his dying face!
The late repentance of that hour,
When Penitence hath lost her power
To tear one terror from the grave—
And will not soothe, and can not save!

        .   .   .   .   .   .

'The cold in clime are cold in blood,
    Their love can scarce deserve the name;   1100
But mine was like the lava flood
    That boils in Ætna's breast of flame.
I cannot prate in puling strain
Of ladye-love, and beauty's chain;
If changing cheek, and scorching vein—
Lips taught to writhe, but not complain—
If bursting heart, and madd'ning brain—
And daring deed, and vengeful steel—
And all that I have felt—and feel—
Betoken love—that love was mine,   1110

And shewn by many a bitter sign.
'Tis true, I could not whine nor sigh,
I knew but to obtain or die.
I die—but first I have possest,
And come what may, I *have been* blest;
Shall I the doom I sought upbraid?
No—reft of all—yet undismay'd
But for the thought of Leila slain,
Give me the pleasure with the pain,
So would I live and love again.   1120
I grieve, but not, my holy guide!
For him who dies, but her who died;
She sleeps beneath the wandering wave—
Ah! had she but an earthly grave,
This breaking heart and throbbing head
Should seek and share her narrow bed.
She was a form of life and light—
That seen—became a part of sight,
And rose—where'er I turned mine eye—
The Morning-star of Memory!   1130

'Yes, Love indeed is light from heaven—
    A spark of that immortal fire
With angels shar'd—by Alla given,
    To lift from earth our low desire.
Devotion wafts the mind above,
But Heaven itself descends in love—
A feeling from the Godhead caught,
To wean from self each sordid thought—
A Ray of him who form'd the whole—
A Glory circling round the soul!   1140
I grant *my* love imperfect—all
That mortals by the name miscall—
Then deem it evil—what thou wilt—
But say, oh say, *hers* was not guilt!
She was my life's unerring light—
That quench'd—what beam shall break my night?
Oh! would it shone to lead me still,
Although to death or deadliest ill!—
Why marvel ye? if they who lose
    This present joy, this future hope,   1150

No more with sorrow meekly cope—
In phrenzy then their fate accuse—
In madness do those fearful deeds
  That seem to add but guilt to woe.
Alas! the breast that inly bleeds
  Hath nought to dread from outward blow—
Who falls from all he knows of bliss,
Cares little into what abyss.—
Fierce as the gloomy vulture's now
  To thee, old man, my deeds appear—   1160
I read abhorrence on thy brow,
  And this too was I born to bear!
'Tis true, that, like that bird of prey,
With havoc have I mark'd my way—
But this was taught me by the dove—
To die—and know no second love.
This lesson yet hath man to learn,
Taught by the thing he dares to spurn—
The bird that sings within the brake,
The swan that swims upon the lake,   1170
One mate, and one alone, will take.
And let the fool still prone to range,
And sneer on all who cannot change—
Partake his jest with boasting boys,
I envy not his varied joys—
But deem such feeble, heartless man,
Less than yon solitary swan—
Far—far beneath the shallow maid
He left believing and betray'd.
Such shame at least was never mine—   1180
Leila—each thought was only thine!—
My good, my guilt, my weal, my woe,
My hope on high—my all below.
Earth holds no other like to thee,
Or if it doth, in vain for me—
For worlds I dare not view the dame
Resembling thee, yet not the same.
The very crimes that mar my youth,
This bed of death—attest my truth—
'Tis all too late—thou wert—thou art   1190
The cherished madness of my heart!

'And she was lost—and yet I breathed,
    But not the breath of human life—
A serpent round my heart was wreathed,
    And stung my every thought to strife.—
Alike all time—abhorred all place,
Shuddering I shrunk from Nature's face,
Where every hue that charmed before
The blackness of my bosom wore:—
The rest—thou dost already know,   1200
And all my sins and half my woe—
But talk no more of penitence,
Thou see'st I soon shall part from hence—
And if thy holy tale were true—
The deed that's done can'st *thou* undo?
Think me not thankless—but this grief
Looks not to priesthood for relief.*
My soul's estate in secret guess—
But would'st thou pity more—say less—
When thou can'st bid my Leila live,   1210
Then will I sue thee to forgive;
Then plead my cause in that high place
Where purchased masses proffer grace—
Go—when the hunter's hand hath wrung
From forest-cave her shrieking young,
And calm the lonely lioness—
But soothe not—mock not *my* distress!

'In early days, and calmer hours,
    When heart with heart delights to blend,
Where bloom my native valley's bowers—   1220
    I had—Ah! have I now?—a friend!—
To him this pledge I charge thee send—
    Memorial of a youthful vow;
I would remind him of my end,—
    Though souls absorbed like mine allow
Brief thought to distant friendship's claim,
Yet dear to him my blighted name.
'Tis strange—he prophesied my doom,
    And I have smil'd—(I then could smile—)
When Prudence would his voice assume,   1230
    And warn—I reck'd not what—the while—

But now remembrance whispers o'er
Those accents scarcely mark'd before.
Say—that his bodings came to pass,
  And he will start to hear their truth,
  And wish his words had not been sooth.
Tell him—unheeding as I was—
  Through many a busy bitter scene
  Of all our golden youth had been—
In pain, my faltering tongue had tried   1240
To bless his memory ere I died;
But heaven in wrath would turn away,
If Guilt should for the guiltless pray.
I do not ask him not to blame—
Too gentle he to wound my name;
And what have I to do with fame?
I do not ask him not to mourn,
Such cold request might sound like scorn;
And what than friendship's manly tear
May better grace a brother's bier?   1250
But bear this ring—his own of old—
And tell him—what thou dost behold!
The wither'd frame, the ruined mind,
The wrack by passion left behind—
A shrivelled scroll, a scatter'd leaf,
Sear'd by the autumn blast of grief!

.   .   .   .   .   .

'Tell me no more of fancy's gleam,
No, father, no, 'twas not a dream;
Alas! the dreamer first must sleep,
I only watch'd, and wish'd to weep;   1260
But could not, for my burning brow
Throbb'd to the very brain as now.
I wish'd but for a single tear,
As something welcome, new, and dear;
I wish'd it then—I wish it still,
Despair is stronger than my will.
Waste not thine orison—despair
Is mightier than thy pious prayer;
I would not, if I might, be blest,

I want no paradise—but rest.   1270
'Twas then, I tell thee, father! then
I saw her—yes—she liv'd again;
And shining in her white symar,*
As through yon pale grey cloud—the star
Which now I gaze on, as on her
Who look'd and looks far lovelier;
Dimly I view its trembling spark—
To-morrow's night shall be more dark—
And I—before its rays appear,
That lifeless thing the living fear.   1280
I wander, father! for my soul
Is fleeting towards the final goal;
I saw her, friar! and I rose,
Forgetful of our former woes;
And rushing from my couch, I dart,
And clasp her to my desperate heart;
I clasp—what is it that I clasp?
No breathing form within my grasp,
No heart that beats reply to mine,
Yet, Leila! yet the form is thine!   1290
And art thou, dearest, chang'd so much,
As meet my eye, yet mock my touch?
Ah! were thy beauties e'er so cold,
I care not—so my arms enfold
The all they ever wish'd to hold.
Alas! around a shadow prest,
They shrink upon my lonely breast;
Yet still—'tis there—in silence stands,
And beckons with beseeching hands!
With braided hair, and bright-black eye—   1300
I knew 'twas false—she could not die!
But he is dead—within the dell
I saw him buried where he fell;
He comes not—for he cannot break
From earth—why then art thou awake?
They told me, wild waves roll'd above
The face I view, the form I love;
They told me—'twas a hideous tale!
I'd tell it—but my tongue would fail—
If true—and from thine ocean-cave   1310

Thou com'st to claim a calmer grave,
Oh! pass thy dewy fingers o'er
This brow that then will burn no more;
Or place them on my hopeless heart—
But, shape or shade!—whate'er thou art,
In mercy, ne'er again depart—
Or farther with thee bear my soul,
Than winds can waft—or waters roll!—

.   .   .   .   .   .

'Such is my name, and such my tale,
    Confessor—to thy secret ear,   1320
I breathe the sorrows I bewail,
    And thank thee for the general tear
This glazing eye could never shed.
Then lay me with the humblest dead,
And save the cross above my head,
Be neither name nor emblem spread
By prying stranger to be read,
Or stay the passing pilgrim's tread.'
He pass'd—nor of his name and race
Hath left a token or a trace,   1330
Save what the father must not say
Who shrived him on his dying day;
This broken tale was all we knew
Of her he lov'd, or him he slew.*

BYRON'S NOTES TO *THE GIAOUR*

l. 3. A tomb above the rocks on the promontory, by some supposed the
    sepulchre of Themistocles.

l. 22. The attachment of the nightingale to the rose is a well-known Persian
    fable. If I mistake not, the 'Bulbul of a thousand tales' is one of his
    appellations.

l. 40. The guitar is the constant amusement of the Greek sailor by night:
    with a steady fair wind, and during a calm, it is accompanied always by
    the voice, and often by dancing.

l. 81.   Ay, but to die and go we know not where,
                          To lie in cold obstruction.
                    [*Measure for Measure*, III.i. [118–19]

l. 89. I trust that few of my readers have ever had an opportunity of witnessing what is here attempted in description, but those who have will probably retain a painful remembrance of that singular beauty which pervades, with few exceptions, the features of the dead, a few hours, and but for a few hours, after 'the spirit is not there'. It is to be remarked in cases of violent death by gun-shot wounds, the expression is always that of languor, whatever the natural energy of the sufferer's character; but in death from a stab the countenance preserves its traits of feeling or ferocity, and the mind its bias, to the last.

l. 151. Athens is the property of the Kislar Aga (the slave of the seraglio and guardian of the women), who appoints the Waywode. A pandar and eunuch—these are not polite, yet true appellations—now *governs* the *governor* of Athens!

l. 190. Infidel.

l. 225. 'Tophaike', musquet.—The Bairam is announced by the cannon at sunset; the illumination of the Mosques, and the firing of all kinds of small arms, loaded with *ball*, proclaim it during the night.

l. 251. Jerreed, or Djerrid, a blunted Turkish Javelin, which is darted from horseback with great force and precision. It is a favourite exercise of the Mussulmans; but I know not if it can be called a *manly* one, since the most expert in the art are the Black Eunuchs of Constantinople.—I think, next to these, a Mamlouk at Smyrna was the most skilful that came within my observation.

l. 282. The blast of the desert, fatal to every thing living, and alluded to in eastern poetry.

l. 343. To partake of food, to break bread and salt with your host, insures the safety of the guest: even though an enemy, his person from that moment is sacred.

l. 351. I need hardly observe, that Charity and Hospitality are the first duties enjoined by Mahomet; and to say truth, very generally practised by his disciples. The first praise that can be bestowed on a chief, is a panegyric on his bounty; the next, on his valour.

l. 355. The ataghan, a long dagger worn with pistols in the belt, in a metal scabbard, generally of silver, and, among the wealthier, gilt, or of gold.

l. 357. Green is the privileged colour of the prophet's numerous pretended descendants; with them, as here, faith (the family inheritance) is supposed to supersede the necessity of good works; they are the worst of a very indifferent brood.

l. 358. Salam aleikoum! aleikoum salam! peace be with you; be with you peace—the salutation reserved for the faithful,—to a Christian, 'Urla-rula', a good journey; or saban hiresem, saban serula; good morn, good even; and sometimes, 'may your end be happy'; are the usual salutes.

l. 389. The blue-winged butterfly of Kashmeer, the most rare and beautiful of the species.

l. 434. Alluding to the dubious suicide of the scorpion, so placed for experiment by gentle philosophers. Some maintain that the position of the sting, when turned towards the head, is merely a convulsive movement; but others have actually brought in the verdict 'Felo de se'. The scorpions are surely interested in a speedy decision of the question; as, if once fairly established as insect Catos, they will probably be allowed to live as long as they think proper, without being martyred for the sake of an hypothesis.

l. 449. The cannon at sunset close the Rhamazan; see note [to l. 225].

l. 468. Phingari, the moon.

l. 479. The celebrated fabulous ruby of Sultan Giamschid, the embellisher of Istakhar: from its splendour, named Schebgerag, 'the torch of night'; also, the 'cup of the sun', etc.—In the first editions 'Giamschid' was written as a word of three syllables, so d'Herbelot has it; but I am told Richardson reduces it to a dissyllable, and writes 'Jamshid'. I have left in the text the orthography of the one with the pronunciation of the other.

l. 483. Al-Sirat, the bridge of breadth less than the thread of a famished spider, over which the Mussulmans must *skate* into Paradise, to which it is the only entrance; but this is not the worst, the river beneath being hell itself, into which, as may be expected, the unskilful and tender of foot contrive to tumble with a 'facilis descensus Averni', not very pleasing in prospect to the next passenger. There is a shorter cut downwards for the Jews and Christians.

l. 488. A vulgar error; the Koran allots at least a third of Paradise to well-behaved women; but by far the greater number of Mussulmans interpret the text their own way, and exclude their moieties from heaven. Being enemies to Platonics, they cannot discern 'any fitness of things' in the souls of the other sex, conceiving them to be superseded by the Houris.

l. 494. An Oriental simile, which may, perhaps, though fairly stolen, be deemed 'plus Arabe qu'en Arabie'.

l. 496. Hyacinthine, in Arabic, 'Sunbul', as common a thought in the eastern poets as it was among the Greeks.

l. 506. 'Franguestan', Circassia.

l. 568. Bismillah—'In the name of God', the commencement of all the chapters of the Koran but one, and of prayer and thanksgiving.

l. 593. A phenomenon not uncommon with an angry Mussulman. In 1809, the Capitan Pacha's whiskers at a diplomatic audience were no less lively with indignation than a tiger cat's, to the horror of all the dragomans; the portentous mustachios twisted, they stood erect of their own accord, and were expected every moment to change their colour, but at last condescended to subside, which, probably, saved more heads than they contained hairs.

l. 603. 'Amaun', quarter, pardon.

l. 612. The 'evil eye', a common superstition in the Levant, and of which the imaginary effects are yet very singular to those who conceive themselves affected.

l. 666. The flowered shawls generally worn by persons of rank.

l. 717. The 'Calpac' is the solid cap or centre part of the headdress; the shawl is wound round it, and forms the turban.

l. 723. The turban, pillar, and inscriptive verse, decorate the tombs of the Osmanlies, whether in the cemetery or the wilderness. In the mountains you frequently pass similar mementos; and on enquiry you are informed that they record some victim of rebellion, plunder, or revenge.

l. 734. 'Alla Hu!' the concluding words of the Meuzzin's call to prayer from the highest gallery on the exterior of the Minaret. On a still evening, when the Muezzin has a fine voice, which is frequently the case, the effect is solemn and beautiful beyond all the bells in Christendom.

l. 743. The following is part of a battle song of the Turks:—'I see—I see a dark-eyed girl of Paradise, and she waves a handkerchief, a kerchief of green; and cries aloud, Come, kiss me, for I love thee,' etc.

l. 748. Monkir and Nekir are the inquisitors of the dead, before whom the corpse undergoes a slight noviciate and preparatory training for damnation. If the answers are none of the clearest, he is hauled up with a scythe and thumped down with a red hot mace till properly seasoned, with a variety of subsidiary probations. The office of these angels is no sinecure; there are but two, and the number of orthodox deceased being in a small proportion to the remainder, their hands are always full.

l. 750. Eblis, the Oriental Prince of Darkness.

l. 755. The Vampire superstition is still general in the Levant. Honest Tournefort tells a long story, which Mr Southey, in the notes on Thalaba, quotes about these 'Vroucolochas', as he calls them. The Romaic term is 'Vardoulacha'. I recollect a whole family being terrified by the scream of a child, which they imagined must proceed from such a visitation. The Greeks never mention the word without horror. I find that 'Broucolokas' is an old legitimate Hellenic appellation—at least is so applied to Arsenius, who, according to the Greeks, was after his death animated by the Devil.—The moderns, however, use the word I mention.

l. 781. The freshness of the face, and the wetness of the lip with blood, are the never-failing signs of a Vampire. The stories told in Hungary and Greece of these foul feeders are singular, and some of them most *incredibly* attested.

l. 951. The pelican is, I believe, the bird so libelled, by the imputation of feeding her chickens with her blood.

l. 1077. This superstition of a second-hearing (for I never met with downright second-sight in the East) fell once under my own observation.— On my third journey to Cape Colonna early in 1811, as we passed through the defile that leads from the hamlet between Keratia and Colonna, I observed Dervish Tahiri riding rather out of the path, and leaning his head upon his hand, as if in pain. I rode up and enquired. 'We are in peril,' he answered. 'What Peril? we are not now in Albania, nor in the passes to Ephesus, Messalunghi, or Lepanto; there are plenty of us, well armed, and the Choriates have not courage to be thieves?'— 'True, Affendi, but nevertheless the shot is ringing in my ears.'—'The shot! not a tophaike has been fired this morning.'—'I hear it notwithstanding—Bom—Bom—as plainly as I hear your voice.'—'Psha.'— 'As you please, Affendi; if it is written, so will it be.' I left this quick-eared predestinarian, and rode up to Basili, his Christian compatriot, whose ears, though not at all prophetic, by no means relished the intelligence. We all arrived at Colonna, remained some hours, and returned leisurely, saying a variety of brilliant things, in more languages than spoiled the building of Babel, upon the mistaken seer. Romaic, Arnaout, Turkish, Italian, and English were all exercised, in various conceits, upon the unfortunate Mussulman. While we were contemplating the beautiful prospect, Dervish was occupied about the columns. I thought he was deranged into an antiquarian, and asked him if he had become a '*Palao-castro*' man: 'No,' said he, 'but these pillars will be useful in making a stand'; and added other remarks, which at least evinced his own belief in his troublesome faculty of *fore-hearing*. On our return to Athens, we heard from Leoné (a prisoner set ashore some days after) of the intended attack of the Mainotes, mentioned, with the cause of its not taking place, in the notes to *Childe Harold*, Canto [11 st. 12]. I was at some pains to question the man, and he described the dresses, arms, and marks of the horses of our party so accurately, that with other circumstances, we could not doubt of *his* having been in 'villainous company', and ourselves in a bad neighbourhood. Dervish became a soothsayer for life, and I dare say is now hearing more musquetry than ever will be fired, to the great refreshment of the Arnaouts of Berat, and his native mountains.—I shall mention one trait more of this singular race. In March 1811, a remarkably stout and active Arnaout came (I believe the 50th on the same errand), to offer himself as an attendant, which was declined: 'Well, Affendi,' quoth he, 'may you live!—you would have found me useful. I shall leave the town for the hills to-morrow, in the winter I return, perhaps you will then receive me.'—Dervish, who was present, remarked as a thing of course, and of no consequence, 'in the mean time he will join the Klephtes' (robbers), which was true to the letter.—If not cut off, they come down in the winter, and pass it unmolested in some town, where they are often as well known as their exploits.

l. 1207. The monk's sermon is omitted. It seems to have had so little effect upon the patient, that it could have no hopes from the reader. It may be sufficient to say, that it was of a customary length (as may be perceived from the interruptions and uneasiness of the penitent), and was delivered in the nasal tone of all orthodox preachers.

l. 1273. 'Symar'—Shroud.

l. 1334. The circumstance to which the above story relates was not very uncommon in Turkey. A few years ago the wife of Muchtar Pacha complained to his father of his son's supposed infidelity; he asked with whom, and she had the barbarity to give in a list of the twelve handsomest women in Yanina. They were seized, fastened up in sacks, and drowned in the lake the same night! One of the guards who was present informed me, that not one of the victims uttered a cry, or shewed a symptom of terror at so sudden a 'wrench from all we know, from all we love'. The fate of Phrosine, the fairest of this sacrifice, is the subject of many a Romaic and Arnaout ditty. The story in the text is one told of a young Venetian many years ago, and now nearly forgotten. I heard it by accident recited by one of the coffee-house story-tellers who abound in the Levant, and sing or recite their narratives. The additions and inter-polations by the translator will be easily distinguished from the rest by the want of Eastern imagery; and I regret that my memory has retained so few fragments of the orignal.

For the contents of some of the notes I am indebted partly to d'Her-belot, and partly to that most eastern, and, as Mr Weber justly entitles it, 'sublime tale', the 'Caliph Vathek'. I do not know from what source the author of that singular volume may have drawn his materials; some of his incidents are to be found in the *Bibliothèque Orientale*; but for correctness of costume, beauty of description, and power of imagination, it far surpasses all European imitations; and bears such marks of original-ity, that those who have visited the East will find some difficulty in believing it to be more than a translation. As an Eastern tale, even Rasselas must bow before it; his 'Happy Valley' will not bear a compari-son with the 'Hall of Eblis'.

from THE CORSAIR

9

Unlike the heroes of each ancient race,
Demons in act, but Gods at least in face,
In Conrad's form seems little to admire,
Though his dark eye-brow shades a glance of fire;
Robust but not Herculean—to the sight
No giant frame sets forth his common height;
Yet, in the whole, who paused to look again,
Saw more than marks the crowd of vulgar men;
They gaze and marvel how—and still confess
That thus it is, but why they cannot guess.   10
Sun-burnt his cheek, his forehead high and pale
The sable curls in wild profusion veil;
And oft perforce his rising lip reveals
The haughtier thought it curbs, but scarce conceals.
Though smooth his voice, and calm his general mien,
Still seems there something he would not have seen:
His features' deepening lines and varying hue
At times attracted, yet perplexed the view,
As if within that murkiness of mind
Worked feelings fearful, and yet undefined;   20
Such might it be—that none could truly tell—
Too close enquiry his stern glance would quell.
There breathe but few whose aspect might defy
The full encounter of his searching eye;
He had the skill, when Cunning's gaze would seek
To probe his heart and watch his changing cheek,
At once the observer's purpose to espy,
And on himself roll back his scrutiny,
Lest he to Conrad rather should betray
Some secret thought, than drag that chief's to day.   30
There was a laughing Devil in his sneer,
That raised emotions both of rage and fear;
And where his frown of hatred darkly fell,
Hope withering fled—and mercy sighed farewell!

10

Slight are the outward signs of evil thought,
Within—within—'twas there the spirit wrought!

Love shows all changes—Hate, Ambition, Guile,
Betray no further than the bitter smile;
The lip's least curl, the lightest paleness thrown
Along the governed aspect, speak alone   40
Of deeper passions; and to judge their mien,
He, who would see, must be himself unseen.
Then—with the hurried tread, the upward eye,
The clenched hand, the pause of agony,
That listens, starting, lest the step too near
Approach intrusive on that mood of fear:
Then—with each feature working from the heart,
With feelings loosed to strengthen—not depart;
That rise—convulse—contend—that freeze, or glow,
Flush in the cheek, or damp upon the brow;   50
Then—Stranger! if thou canst, and tremblest not,
Behold his soul—the rest that soothes his lot!
Mark—how that lone and blighted bosom sears
The scathing thought of execrated years!
Behold—but who hath seen, or e'er shall see,
Man as himself—the secret spirit free?

II

Yet was not Conrad thus by Nature sent
To lead the guilty—guilt's worst instrument—
His soul was changed, before his deeds had driven
Him forth to war with man and forfeit heaven.   60
Warped by the world in Disappointment's school,
In words too wise, in conduct *there* a fool;
Too firm to yield, and far too proud to stoop,
Doomed by his very virtues for a dupe,
He cursed those virtues as the cause of ill,
And not the traitors who betrayed him still;
Nor deemed that gifts bestowed on better men
Had left him joy, and means to give again.
Feared—shunned—belied—ere youth had lost her force,
He hated man too much to feel remorse,   70
And thought the voice of wrath a sacred call,
To pay the injuries of some on all.
He knew himself a villain—but he deemed
The rest no better than the thing he seemed;

And scorned the best as hypocrites who hid
Those deeds the bolder spirit plainly did.
He knew himself detested, but he knew
The hearts that loathed him, crouched and dreaded too.
Lone, wild, and strange, he stood alike exempt
From all affection and from all contempt: 80
His name could sadden, and his acts surprise;
But they that feared him dared not to despise:
Man spurns the worm, but pauses ere he wake
The slumbering venom of the folded snake:
The first may turn—but not avenge the blow;
The last expires—but leaves no living foe;
Fast to the doomed offender's form it clings,
And he may crush—not conquer—still it stings!

                              12

None are all evil—quickening round his heart,
One softer feeling would not yet depart.   90
Oft could he sneer at others as beguiled
By passions worthy of a fool or child;
Yet 'gainst that passion vainly still he strove,
And even in him it asks the name of Love!
Yes, it was love—unchangeable—unchanged,
Felt but for one from whom he never ranged;
Though fairest captives daily met his eye,
He shunned, nor sought, but coldly passed them by;
Though many a beauty drooped in prisoned bower,
None ever soothed his most unguarded hour.   100
Yes—it was Love—if thoughts of tenderness,
Tried in temptation, strengthened by distress,
Unmoved by absence, firm in every clime,
And yet—Oh more than all!—untired by time;
Which nor defeated hope, not baffled wile,
Could render sullen were she ne'er to smile,
Nor rage could fire, nor sickness fret to vent
On her one murmur of his discontent;
Which still would meet with joy, with calmness part,
Lest that his look of grief should reach her heart;   110
Which nought removed, nor menaced to remove
If there be love in mortals—this was love!

He was a villain—ay—reproaches shower
On him—but not the passion, nor its power,
Which only proved, all other virtues gone,
Not guilt itself could quench this loveliest one!

[1814]

from *LARA*

17

In him inexplicably mix'd appeared
Much to be loved and hated, sought and feared;
Opinion varying o'er his hidden lot,
In praise or railing ne'er his name forgot;
His silence formed a theme for others' prate—
They guess'd—they gazed—they fain would know
    his fate.
What had he been? what was he, thus unknown,
Who walked their world, his lineage only known?
A hater of his kind? yet some would say,
With them he could seem gay amidst the gay;   10
But own'd, that smile if oft observed and near,
Waned in its mirth and withered to a sneer;
That smile might reach his lip, but passed not by,
None e'er could trace its laughter to his eye:
Yet there was softness too in his regard,
At times, a heart as not by nature hard,
But once perceiv'd, his spirit seem'd to chide
Such weakness, as unworthy of its pride,
And steel'd himself, as scorning to redeem
One doubt from others' half withheld esteem;   20
In self-inflicted penance of a breast
Which tenderness might once have wrung from rest;
In vigilance of grief that would compel
The soul to hate for having lov'd too well.

18

There was in him a vital scorn of all:
As if the worst had fall'n which could befall

He stood a stranger in this breathing world,
An erring spirit from another hurled;
A thing of dark imaginings, that shaped
By choice the perils he by chance escaped;   30
But 'scaped in vain, for in their memory yet
His mind would half exult and half regret:
With more capacity for love than earth
Bestows on most of mortal mould and birth,
His early dreams of good outstripp'd the truth,
And troubled manhood followed baffled youth;
With thought of years in phantom chase misspent,
And wasted powers for better purpose lent;
And fiery passions that had poured their wrath
In hurried desolation o'er his path,   40
And left the better feelings all at strife
In wild reflection o'er his stormy life;
But haughty still, and loth himself to blame,
He called on Nature's self to share the shame,
And charged all faults upon the fleshly form
She gave to clog the soul, and feast the worm;
'Till he at last confounded good and ill,
And half mistook for fate the acts of will:
Too high for common selfishness, he could
At times resign his own for others' good,   50
But not in pity, not because he ought,
But in some strange perversity of thought,
That swayed him onward with a secret pride
To do what few or none would do beside;
And this same impulse would in tempting time
Mislead his spirit equally to crime;
So much he soared beyond, or sunk beneath
The men with whom he felt condemned to breathe,
And longed by good or ill to separate
Himself from all who shared his mortal state;   60
His mind abhorring this had fixed her throne
Far from the world, in regions of her own;
Thus coldly passing all that passed below,
His blood in temperate seeming now would flow:
Ah! happier if it ne'er with guilt had glowed,
But ever in that icy smoothness flowed!
'Tis true, with other men their path he walked,

And like the rest in seeming did and talked,
Nor outraged Reason's rules by flaw nor start,
His madness was not of the head, but heart;   70
And rarely wandered in his speech, or drew
His thoughts so forth as to offend the view.

19

With all that chilling mystery of mien,
And seeming gladness to remain unseen;
He had (if 'twere not nature's boon) an art
Of fixing memory on another's heart:
It was not love perchance—nor hate—nor aught
That words can image to express the thought;
But they who saw him did not see in vain,
And once beheld, would ask of him again: 80
And those to whom he spake remembered well,
And on the words, however light, would dwell:
None knew, nor how, nor why, but he entwined
Himself perforce around the hearer's mind;
There he was stamp'd, in liking, or in hate,
If greeted once; however brief the date
That friendship, pity, or aversion knew,
Still there within the inmost thought he grew.
You could not penetrate his soul, but found,
Despite your wonder, to your own he wound;   90
His presence haunted still; and from the breast
He forced an all unwilling interest;
Vain was the struggle in that mental net,
His spirit seemed to dare you to forget!

[1814]

Stanzas for Music

I speak not—I trace not—I breathe not thy name,
There is grief in the sound—there were guilt in the fame;
But the tear which now burns on my cheek may impart
The deep thought that dwells in that silence of heart.

Too brief for our passion, too long for our peace,
Were those hours, can their joy or their bitterness cease?
We repent—we abjure—we will break from our chain;
We must part—we must fly to—unite it again.

Oh! thine be the gladness and mine be the guilt,
Forgive me adored one—forsake if thou wilt;
But the heart which I bear shall expire undebased,
And man shall not break it—whatever thou may'st.

And stern to the haughty, but humble to thee,
My soul in its bitterest blackness shall be;
And our days seem as swift—and our moments more
  sweet,
With thee by my side—than the world at our feet.

One sigh of thy sorrow—one look of thy love,
Shall turn me or fix, shall reward or reprove;
And the heartless may wonder at all we resign,
Thy lip shall reply not to them—but to mine.

[1814]

They Say that Hope is Happiness

'Felix qui potuit rerum cognoscere causas.'
VIRGIL

1

They say that Hope is happiness—
  But genuine Love must prize the past;
And Mem'ry wakes the thoughts that bless:
  They rose the first—they set the last.

2

And all that mem'ry loves the most
  Was once our only hope to be:
And all that hope adored and lost
  Hath melted into memory.

3

Alas! it is delusion all—
   The future cheats us from afar: 10
Nor can we be what we recall,
   Nor dare we think on what we are.

          [1814]

Stanzas for Music

O Lachrymarum fons, tenero sacros
Ducentium ortus ex animo: quater
Felix! in imo qui scatentem
Pectore te, pia Nympha, sensit.

         Gray's Poemata

1

There's not a joy the world can give like that it takes away,
When the glow of early thought declines in feeling's dull
    decay;
'Tis not on youth's smooth cheek the blush alone, which fades
    so fast,
But the tender bloom of heart is gone, ere youth itself be
    past.

2

Then the few whose spirits float above the wreck of happiness,
Are driven o'er the shoals of guilt or ocean of excess:
The magnet of their course is gone, or only points in vain
The shore to which their shiver'd sail shall never stretch
    again.

3

Then the mortal coldness of the soul like death itself comes
    down;
It cannot feel for others' woes, it dare not dream its own;   10
That heavy chill has frozen o'er the fountain of our tears,
And tho' the eye may sparkle still, 'tis where the ice appears.

4

Tho' wit may flash from fluent lips, and mirth distract the
    breast,
Through midnight hours that yield no more their former hope
    of rest;
'Tis but as ivy-leaves around the ruin'd turret wreath,
All green and wildly fresh without but worn and grey beneath.

5

Oh could I feel as I have felt,—or be what I have been,
Or weep as I could once have wept, o'er many a vanished
    scene:
As springs in deserts found seem sweet, all brackish though
    they be,
So midst the wither'd waste of life, those tears would flow to
    me.   20

[1815]

She Walks in Beauty

1

She walks in beauty, like the night
    Of cloudless climes and starry skies;
And all that's best of dark and bright
    Meet in her aspect and her eyes:
Thus mellow'd to that tender light
    Which heaven to gaudy day denies.

2

One shade the more, one ray the less,
    Had half impair'd the nameless grace
Which waves in every raven tress,
    Or softly lightens o'er her face;   10
Where thoughts serenely sweet express
    How pure, how dear their dwelling place.

3

And on that cheek, and o'er that brow,
    So soft, so calm, yet eloquent,
The smiles that win, the tints that glow,
    But tell of days in goodness spent,
A mind at peace with all below,
    A heart whose love is innocent!

[1815]

Sun of the Sleepless!

Sun of the sleepless! melancholy star!
Whose tearful beam glows tremulously far,
That show'st the darkness thou canst not dispel,
How like art thou to joy remembered well!
So gleams the past, the light of other days,
Which shines, but warms not with its powerless rays;
A night-beam Sorrow watcheth to behold,
Distinct, but distant—clear—but, oh how cold!

[1815]

The Destruction of Semnacherib

1

The Assyrian came down like the wolf on the fold,
And his cohorts were gleaming in purple and gold;
And the sheen of their spears was like stars on the sea,
When the blue wave rolls nightly on deep Galilee.

2

Like the leaves of the forest when Summer is green,
That host with their banners at sunset were seen:
Like the leaves of the forest when Autumn hath blown,
That host on the morrow lay withered and strown.

3

For the Angel of Death spread his wings on the blast,
And breathed in the face of the foe as he pass'd;   10
And the eyes of the sleepers wax'd deadly and chill,
And their hearts but once heaved, and for ever grew still!

4

And there lay the steed with his nostril all wide,
But through it there roll'd not the breath of his pride:
And the foam of his gasping lay white on the turf,
And cold as the spray of the rock-beating surf.

5

And there lay the rider distorted and pale,
With the dew on his brow, and the rust on his mail;
And the tents were all silent, the banners alone,
The lances unlifted, the trumpet unblown.   20

6

And the widows of Ashur are loud in their wail,
And the idols are broke in the temple of Baal;
And the might of the Gentle, unsmote by the sword,
Hath melted like snow in the glance of the Lord!

[1815]

When We Two Parted

I

When we two parted
    In silence and tears,
Half broken-hearted
    To sever for years,
Pale grew thy cheek and cold,
    Colder thy kiss;
Truly that hour foretold
    Sorrow to this.

2

The dew of the morning
  Sunk chill on my brow—
It felt like the warning
  Of what I feel now.
Thy vows are all broken,
  And light is thy fame;
I hear thy name spoken,
  And share in its shame.

3

They name thee before me,
  A knell to mine ear;
A shudder comes o'er me—
  Why wert thou so dear?
They know not I knew thee,
  Who knew thee too well:—
Long, long shall I rue thee,
  Too deeply to tell.

4

In secret we met—
  In silence I grieve,
That thy heart could forget,
  Thy spirit deceive.
If I should meet thee
  After long years,
How should I greet thee!—
  With silence and tears.

Fare Thee Well!

Alas! they had been friends in Youth;
But whispering tongues can poison truth;
And constancy lives in realms above:
And Life is thorny; and youth is vain:
And to be wroth with one we love,
Doth work like madness in the brain:

. . . . .

But never either found another
To free the hollow heart from paining—
They stood aloof, the scars remaining,
Like cliffs, which had been rent asunder;
A dreary sea now flows between,
But neither heat, nor frost, nor thunder
Shall wholly do away, I ween,
The marks of that which once hath been.

Coleridge's Christabel [408–13, 419–26]

Fare thee well! and if for ever—
  Still for ever, fare *thee well*—
Even though unforgiving, never
  'Gainst thee shall my heart rebel.—
Would that breast were bared before thee
  Where thy head so oft hath lain,
While that placid sleep came o'er thee
  Which thou ne'er can'st know again:
Would that breast by thee glanc'd over,
  Every inmost thought could show!   10
Then, thou wouldst at last discover
  'Twas not well to spurn it so—
Though the world for this commend thee—
  Though it smile upon the blow,
Even its praises must offend thee,
  Founded on another's woe—
Though my many faults defaced me,
  Could no other arm be found
Than the one which once embraced me,
  To inflict a cureless wound!   20
Yet—oh, yet—thyself deceive not—

Love may sink by slow decay,
But by sudden wrench, believe not,
   Hearts can thus be torn away;
Still thine own its life retaineth—
   Still must mine—though bleeding—beat,
And the undying thought which paineth
   Is—that we no more may meet.—
These are words of deeper sorrow
   Than the wail above the dead,
Both shall live—but every morrow   30
   Wake us from a widowed bed.—
And when thou wouldst solace gather—
   When our child's first accents flow—
Wilt thou teach her to say—'Father!'
   Though his care she must forgo?
When her little hands shall press thee—
   When her lip to thine is prest—
Think of him whose prayer shall bless thee—
   Think of him thy love had bless'd.   40
Should her lineaments resemble
   Those thou never more may'st see—
Then thy heart will softly tremble
   With a pulse yet true to me.—
All my faults—perchance thou knowest—
   All my madness—none can know;
All my hopes—where'er thou goest—
   Wither—yet with *thee* they go.—
Every feeling hath been shaken,
   Pride—which not a world could bow—   50
Bows to thee—by thee forsaken
   Even my soul forsakes me now.—
But 'tis done—all words are idle—
   Words from me are vainer still;
But the thoughts we cannot bridle
   Force their way without the will.—
Fare thee well!—thus disunited—
   Torn from every nearer tie—
Seared in heart—and lone—and blighted—
   More than this, I scarce can die.   60

[1816]

[*A Fragment*]

Could I remount the river of my years
To the first fountain of our smiles and tears
I would not trace again its stream of hours
Between its outworn banks of withered flowers.
But bid it flow as now—until it glides
Into the number of the nameless tides.
What is this death—a quiet of the heart—
The whole of that of which we are a part—
For life is but a vision—what I see
Of all which lives alone is life to me   10
And being so—the Absent are the dead
Who haunt us from tranquillity—and spread
A dreary shroud around us—and invest
With sad remembrancers our hours of rest.
The absent are the dead,—for they are cold,
And ne'er can be what once we did behold—
And they are changed—and cheerless—or if yet
The unforgotten do not all forget—
Since thus divided—equal must it be
If the deep barrier be of earth or sea—   20
It may be both,—but one day end it must
In the dark union of insensate dust.
The underearth inhabitants—are they
But mingled millions decomposed to clay—
The ashes of a thousand Ages spread
Wherever Man has trodden or shall tread—
Or do they in their silent cities dwell
Each in his incommunicative cell—
Or have they their own language—and a sense
Of breathless being—darkened and intense—   30
As midnight in her solitude—Oh Earth!
Where are the past—and wherefore had they birth?
The dead are thy inheritors—and we
But bubbles on thy surface:—and the key
Of thy profundity is in the grave,
The portal of thy universal cave—
Where I would walk in Spirit—and behold

Our elements resolved to things untold,
And fathom hidden wonders—and explore
The essence of great bosoms now no more.   40

[1816]

Prometheus

1

Titan! To whose immortal eyes
   The sufferings of mortality,
   Seen in their sad reality,
Were not as things that gods despise;
What was thy pity's recompense?
A silent suffering, and intense;
The rock, the vulture, and the chain,
All that the proud can feel of pain,
The agony they do not show,
The suffocating sense of woe,   10
   Which speaks but in its loneliness,
And then is jealous lest the sky
Should have a listener, nor will sigh
   Until its voice is echoless.

2

Titan! to thee the strife was given
   Between the suffering and the will,
   Which torture where they cannot kill;
And the inexorable Heaven,
And the deaf tyranny of Fate,
The ruling principle of Hate,
Which for its pleasure doth create   20
The things it may annihilate,
Refused thee even the boon to die:
The wretched gift eternity
Was thine—and thou hast borne it well.
All that the Thunderer wrung from thee
Was but the menace which flung back
On him the torments of thy rack;

The fate thou didst so well foresee
But would not to appease him tell;   30
And in thy Silence was his Sentence,
And in his Soul a vain repentance,
And evil dread so ill dissembled
That in his hand the lightnings trembled.

                    3
Thy Godlike crime was to be kind,
To render with thy precepts less
The sum of human wretchedness,
And strengthen Man with his own mind;
But baffled as thou wert from high,
Still in thy patient energy,   40
In the endurance, and repulse
Of thine impenetrable Spirit,
Which Earth and Heaven could not convulse,
A mighty lesson we inherit:
Thou art a symbol and a sign
To Mortals of their fate and force;
Like thee, Man is in part divine,
A troubled stream from a pure source;
And Man in portions can foresee
His own funereal destiny;   50
His wretchedness, and his resistance,
And his sad unallied existence:
To which his Spirit may oppose
Itself—an equal to all woes,
And a firm will, and a deep sense,
Which even in torture can descry
Its own concentred recompense,
Triumphant where it dares defy,
And making Death a Victory.

                                          [1817]

Stanzas to [*Augusta*]

1

Though the day of my destiny's over,
 And the star of my fate hath declined,
Thy soft heart refused to discover
 The faults which so many could find;
Though thy soul with my grief was acquainted,
 It shrunk not to share it with me,
And the love which my spirit hath painted
 It never hath found but in *thee*.

2

Then when nature around me is smiling
 The last smile which answers to mine,   10
I do not believe it beguiling
 Because it reminds me of thine;
And when winds are at war with the ocean,
 As the breasts I believed in with me,
If their billows excite an emotion
 It is that they bear me from *thee*.

3

Though the rock of my last hope is shiver'd,
 And its fragments are sunk in the wave,
Though I feel that my soul is deliver'd
 To pain—it shall not be its slave.   20
There is many a pang to pursue me:
 They may crush, but they shall not contemn—
They may torture, but shall not subdue me—
 'Tis of *thee* that I think—not of them.

4

Thou human, thou didst not deceive me,
 Though woman, thou didst not forsake,
Though loved, thou foreborest to grieve me,
 Though slander'd, thou never could'st shake,—

Though trusted, thou didst not betray me,
   Though parted, it was not to fly,   30
Though watchful, 'twas not to defame me,
   Nor, mute, that the world might belie.

5

Yet I blame not the world, nor despise it,
   Nor the war of the many with one—
If my soul was not fitted to prize it
   'Twas folly not sooner to shun:
And if dearly that error hath cost me,
   And more than I once could foresee,
I have found that, whatever it lost me,
   It could not deprive me of *thee*.   40

6

From the wreck of my past, which hath perish'd,
   Thus much I at least may recall,
It hath taught me that what I most cherish'd
   Deserved to be dearest of all:
In the desert a fountain is springing,
   In the wide waste there still is a tree,
And a bird in the solitude singing,
   Which speaks to my spirit of *thee*.

                      [1817]

[*Epistle to Augusta*]

1

My Sister—my sweet Sister—if a name
   Dearer and purer were—it should be thine.
Mountains and Seas divide us—but I claim
   No tears—but tenderness to answer mine:
Go where I will, to me thou art the same—
   A loved regret which I would not resign—
There yet are two things in my destiny
A world to roam through—and a home with thee.

2

The first were nothing—had I still the last
   It were the haven of my happiness—   10
But other claims and other ties thou hast—
   And mine is not the wish to make them less.
A strange doom was thy father's son's and past
   Recalling—as it lies beyond redress—
Reversed for him our grandsire's fate of yore
He had no rest at sea—nor I on shore.

3

If my inheritance of storms hath been
   In other elements—and on the rocks
Of perils overlooked or unforeseen
   I have sustained my share of worldly shocks   20
The fault was mine—nor do I seek to screen
   My errors with defensive paradox—
I have been cunning in mine overthrow
The careful pilot of my proper woe.

4

Mine were my faults—and mine be their reward—
   My whole life was a contest—since the day
That gave me being gave me that which marred
   The gift—a fate or will that walked astray—
And I at times have found the struggle hard
   And thought of shaking off my bonds of clay—   30
But now I fain would for a time survive
If but to see what next can well arrive.

5

Kingdoms and empires in my little day
   I have outlived and yet I am not old—
And when I look on this, the petty spray
   Of my own years of trouble, which have rolled
Like a wild bay of breakers, melts away:—
   Something—I know no what—does still uphold
A spirit of slight patience;—not in vain
Even for its own sake do we purchase pain.   40

6

Perhaps—the workings of defiance stir
   Within me,—or perhaps a cold despair—
Brought on when ills habitually recur,—
   Perhaps a harder clime—or purer air—
For to all such may change of soul refer—
   And with light armour we may learn to bear—
Have taught me a strange quiet—which was not
The chief companion of a calmer lot.

7

I feel almost at times as I have felt
   In happy childhood—trees and flowers and brooks   50
Which do remember me of where I dwelt
   Ere my young mind was sacrificed to books—
Come as of yore upon me—and can melt
   My heart with recognition of their looks—
And even at moments I could think I see
Some living things to love—but none like thee.

8

Here are the Alpine landscapes—which create
   A fund for contemplation—to admire
Is a brief feeling of a trivial date—
   But something worthier do such scenes inspire: 60
Here to be lonely is not desolate—
   For much I view which I could most desire—
And above all a lake I can behold—
Lovelier—not dearer—than our own of old.

9

Oh that thou wert but with me!—but I grow
   The fool of my own wishes—and forget
The solitude which I have vaunted so
   Has lost its praise in this but one regret—
There may be others which I less may show—
   I am not of the plaintive mood—and yet   70
I feel an ebb in my philosophy
And the tide rising in my altered eye.

10

I did remind thee of our own dear lake
   By the old Hall which may be mine no more—
Leman's is fair—but think not I forsake
   The sweet remembrance of a dearer shore—
Sad havoc Time must with my memory make
   Ere *that* or *thou* can fade these eyes before—
Though like all things which I have loved—they are
Resigned for ever—or divided far.   80

11

The world is all before me—I but ask
   Of Nature that with which she will comply—
It is but in her Summer's sun to bask—
   To mingle in the quiet of her sky—
To see her gentle face without a mask
   And never gaze on it with apathy—
She was my early friend—and now shall be
My Sister—till I look again on thee.

12

I can reduce all feelings but this one
   And that I would not—for at length I see   90
Such scenes as those wherein my life begun
   The earliest—were the only paths for me.
Had I but sooner known the crowd to shun
   I had been better than I now can be
The passions which have torn me would have slept—
I had not suffered—and *thou* hadst not wept.

13

With false Ambition what had I to do?
   Little with love, and least of all with fame!
And yet they came unsought and with me grew,
   And made me all which they can make—a Name.   100
Yet this was not the end I did pursue—
   Surely I once beheld a nobler aim.
But all is over—I am one the more
To baffled millions which have gone before.

14

And for the future—this world's future may
   From me demand but little from my care;
I have outlived myself by many a day,
   Having survived so many things that were—
My years have been no slumber—but the prey
   Of ceaseless vigils;—for I had the share   110
Of life which might have filled a century
Before its fourth in time had passed me by.

15

And for the remnants which may be to come
   I am content—and for the past I feel
Not thankless—for within the crowded sum
   Of struggles—happiness at times would steal—
And for the present—I would not benumb
   My feelings farther—nor shall I conceal
That with all this I still can look around
And worship Nature with a thought profound.   120

16

For thee—my own sweet Sister—in thy heart
   I know myself secure—as thou in mine
We were and are—I am—even as thou art—
   Beings—who ne'er each other can resign
It is the same together or apart—
   From life's commencement to its slow decline—
We are entwined—let death come slow or fast—
The tie which bound the first endures the last.—

         [1816]

Darkness

I had a dream, which was not all a dream.
The bright sun was extinguish'd, and the stars
Did wander darkling in the eternal space,
Rayless, and pathless, and the icy earth
Swung blind and blackening in the moonless air;
Morn came, and went—and came, and brought no day,
And men forgot their passions in the dread
Of this their desolation; and all hearts
Were chill'd into a selfish prayer for light:
And they did live by watchfires—and the thrones,   10
The palaces of crowned kings—the huts,
The habitations of all things which dwell,
Were burnt for beacons; cities were consumed,
And men were gathered round their blazing homes
To look once more into each other's face;
Happy were those who dwelt within the eye
Of the volcanos, and their mountain-torch:
A fearful hope was all the world contain'd;
Forests were set on fire—but hour by hour
They fell and faded—and the crackling trunks   20
Extinguish'd with a crash—and all was black.
The brows of men by the despairing light
Wore an unearthly aspect, as by fits
The flashes fell upon them; some lay down
And hid their eyes and wept; and some did rest
Their chins upon their clenched hands, and smiled;
And others hurried to and fro, and fed
Their funeral piles with fuel, and looked up
With mad disquietude on the dull sky,
The pall of a past world; and then again   30
With curses cast them down upon the dust,
And gnash'd their teeth and howl'd: the wild birds shriek'd,
And, terrified, did flutter on the ground,
And flap their useless wings; the wildest brutes
Came tame and tremulous; and vipers crawl'd
And twined themselves among the multitude,

Hissing, but stingless—they were slain for food:
And War, which for a moment was no more,
Did glut himself again;—a meal was bought
With blood, and each sate sullenly apart   40
Gorging himself in gloom: no love was left;
All earth was but one thought—and that was death,
Immediate and inglorious; and the pang
Of famine fed upon all entrails—men
Died, and their bones were tombless as their flesh;
The meagre by the meagre were devoured,
Even dogs assail'd their masters, all save one,
And he was faithful to a corse, and kept
The birds and beasts and famish'd men at bay,
Till hunger clung them, or the dropping dead   50
Lured their lank jaws; himself sought out no food,
But with a piteous and perpetual moan
And a quick desolate cry, licking the hand
Which answered not with a caress—he died.
The crowd was famish'd by degrees; but two
Of an enormous city did survive,
And they were enemies; they met beside
The dying embers of an altar-place
Where had been heap'd a mass of holy things
For an unholy usage; they raked up,   60
And shivering scraped with their cold skeleton hands
The feeble ashes, and their feeble breath
Blew for a little life, and made a flame
Which was a mockery; then they lifted up
Their eyes as it grew lighter, and beheld
Each other's aspects—saw, and shriek'd, and died—
Even of their mutual hideousness they died,
Unknowing who he was upon whose brow
Famine had written Fiend. The world was void,
The populous and the powerful—was a lump,   70
Seasonless, herbless, treeless, manless, lifeless—
A lump of death—a chaos of hard clay.
The rivers, lakes, and ocean all stood still,
And nothing stirred within their silent depths;
Ships sailorless lay rotting on the sea,
And their masts fell down piecemeal; as they dropp'd
They slept on the abyss without a surge—

The waves were dead; the tides were in their grave,
The moon their mistress had expired before;
The winds were withered in the stagnant air,　　　　　80
And the clouds perish'd; Darkness had no need
Of aid from them—She was the universe.

[1817]

from CHILDE HAROLD'S PILGRIMAGE.
CANTO III

34

There is a very life in our despair,
Vitality of poison,—a quick root
Which feeds these deadly branches; for it were
As nothing did we die; but Life will suit
Itself to Sorrow's most detested fruit,
Like to the apples on the Dead Sea's shore,
All ashes to the taste: Did man compute
Existence by enjoyment, and count o'er
Such hours 'gainst years of life,—say, would he name
　　　threescore?

35

The Psalmist numbered out the years of man:　　　10
They are enough; and if thy tale be *true*,
Thou, who didst grudge him even that fleeting span,
More than enough, thou fatal Waterloo!
Millions of tongues record thee, and anew
Their children's lips shall echo them, and say—
'Here, where the sword united nations drew,
Our countrymen were warring on that day!'
And this is much, and all which will not pass away.

36

There sunk the greatest, nor the worst of men,
Whose spirit antithetically mixt　　　　　20
One moment of the mightiest, and again
On little objects with like firmness fixt,

Extreme in all things! hadst thou been betwixt,
Thy throne had still been thine, or never been;
For daring made thy rise as fall: thou seek'st
Even now to re-assume the imperial mien,
And shake again the world, the Thunderer of the scene!

37

Conqueror and captive of the earth art thou!
She trembles at thee still, and thy wild name
Was ne'er more bruited in men's minds than now   30
That thou art nothing, save the jest of Fame,
Who wooed thee once, thy vassal, and became
The flatterer of thy fierceness, till thou wert
A god unto thyself; nor less the same
To the astounded kingdoms all inert,
Who deem'd thee for a time whate'er thou didst assert.

38

Oh, more or less than man—in high or low,
Battling with nations, flying from the field;
Now making monarchs' necks thy footstool, now
More than thy meanest soldier taught to yield;   40
An empire thou couldst crush, command, rebuild,
But govern not thy pettiest passion, nor,
However deeply in men's spirits skill'd,
Look through thine own, nor curb the lust of war,
Nor learn that tempted Fate will leave the loftiest star.

39

Yet well thy soul hath brook'd the turning tide
With that untaught innate philosophy,
Which, be it wisdom, coldness, or deep pride,
Is gall and wormwood to an enemy.
When the whole host of hatred stood hard by,   50
To watch and mock thee shrinking, thou hast smiled
With a sedate and all-enduring eye;—
When Fortune fled her spoil'd and favourite child,
He stood unbowed beneath the ills upon him piled.

40

Sager than in thy fortunes; for in them
Ambition steel'd thee on too far to show
That just habitual scorn which could contemn
Men and their thoughts; 'twas wise to feel, not so
To wear it ever on thy lip and brow,
And spurn the instruments thou wert to use   60
Till they were turn'd unto thine overthrow:
'Tis but a worthless world to win or lose;
So hath it proved to thee, and all such lot who choose.

41

If, like a tower upon a headlong rock,
Thou hadst been made to stand or fall alone,
Such scorn of man had help'd to brave the shock;
But men's thoughts were the steps which paved thy throne,
Their admiration thy best weapon shone;
The part of Philip's son was thine, not then
(Unless aside thy purple had been thrown)   70
Like stern Diogenes to mock at men;
For sceptred cynics earth were far too wide a den.

42

But quiet to quick bosoms is a hell,
And *there* hath been thy bane; there is a fire
And motion of the soul which will not dwell
In its own narrow being, but aspire
Beyond the fitting medium of desire;
And, but once kindled, quenchless evermore,
Preys upon high adventure, nor can tire
Of aught but rest; a fever at the core,   80
Fatal to him who bears, to all who ever bore.

43

This makes the madmen who have made men mad
By their contagion; Conquerors and Kings,
Founders of sects and systems, to whom add
Sophists, Bards, Statesmen, all unquiet things
Which stir too strongly the soul's secret springs,

And are themselves the fools to those they fool;
Envied, yet how unenviable! what stings
Are theirs! One breast laid open were a school
Which would unteach mankind the lust to shine or rule: 90

44

Their breath is agitation, and their life
A storm whereon they ride, to sink at last,
And yet so nurs'd and bigotted to strife,
That should their days, surviving perils past,
Melt to calm twilight, they feel overcast
With sorrow and supineness, and so die;
Even as a flame unfed, which runs to waste
With its own flickering, or a sword laid by
Which eats into itself, and rusts ingloriously.

45

He who ascends to mountain-tops, shall find   100
The loftiest peaks most wrapt in clouds and snow;
He who surpasses or subdues mankind,
Must look down on the hate of those below.
Though high *above* the sun of glory glow,
And far *beneath* the earth and ocean spread,
Round him are icy rocks, and loudly blow
Contending tempests on his naked head,
And thus reward the toils which to those summits led.

. . . .

77

Here the self-torturing sophist, wild Rousseau,
The apostle of affliction, he who threw   110
Enchantment over passion, and from woe
Wrung overwhelming eloquence, first drew
The breath which made him wretched; yet he knew
How to make madness beautiful, and cast
O'er erring deeds and thoughts, a heavenly hue
Of words, like sunbeams, dazzling as they past
The eyes, which o'er them shed tears feelingly and fast.

78

His love was passion's essence—as a tree
On fire by lightning; with ethereal flame
Kindled he was, and blasted; for to be   120
Thus, and enamoured, were in him the same.
But his was not the love of living dame,
Nor of the dead who rise upon our dreams,
But of ideal beauty, which became
In him existence, and o'erflowing teems
Along his burning page, distempered though it seems.

79

This breathed itself to life in Julie, *this*
Invested her with all that's wild and sweet;
This hallowed, too, the memorable kiss
Which every morn his fevered lip would greet,   130
From hers, who but with friendship his would meet;
But to that gentle touch, through brain and breast
Flash'd the thrill'd spirit's love-devouring heat;
In that absorbing sigh perchance more blest,
Than vulgar minds may be with all they seek possess.

80

His life was one long war with self-sought foes,
Or friends by him self-banish'd; for his mind
Had grown Suspicion's sanctuary, and chose
For its own cruel sacrifice, the kind,
'Gainst whom he raged with fury strange and blind.   140
But he was phrenzied,—wherefore, who may know?
Since cause might be which skill could never find;
But he was phrenzied by disease or woe,
To that worst pitch of all, which wears a reasoning show.

81

For then he was inspired, and from him came,
As from the Pythian's mystic cave of yore,
Those oracles which set the world in flame,
Nor ceased to burn till kingdoms were no more:
Did he not this for France? which lay before

Bowed to the inborn tyranny of years? 150
Broken and trembling, to the yoke she bore,
  Till by the voice of him and his compeers,
Roused up to too much wrath which follows o'ergrown fears?

82

They made themselves a fearful monument!
The wreck of old opinions—things which grew
Breathed from the birth of time: the veil they rent,
And what behind it lay, all earth shall view.
But good with ill they also overthrew,
Leaving but ruins, wherewith to rebuild
  Upon the same foundation, and renew 160
  Dungeons and thrones, which the same hour re-fill'd,
As heretofore, because ambition was self-will'd.

83

But this will not endure, nor be endured!
Mankind have felt their strength, and made it felt.
They might have used it better, but, allured
By their new vigour, sternly have they dealt
On one another; pity ceased to melt
With her once natural charities. But they,
  Who in oppression's darkness caved had dwelt,
  They were not eagles, nourish'd with the day; 170
What marvel then, at times, if they mistook their prey?

84

What deep wounds ever closed without a scar?
The heart's bleed longest, and but heal to wear
That which disfigures it; and they who war
With their own hopes, and have been vanquish'd, bear
Silence, but not submission: in his lair
Fix'd Passion holds his breath, until the hour
  Which shall atone for years; none need despair:
  It came, it cometh, and will come,—the power
To punish or forgive—in *one* we shall be slower. 180

85

Clear, placid Leman! thy contrasted lake,
With the wild world I dwelt in, is a thing
Which warns me, with its stillness, to forsake
Earth's troubled waters for a purer spring.
This quiet sail is as a noiseless wing
To waft me from distraction; once I loved
Torn ocean's roar, but thy soft murmuring
Sounds sweet as if a sister's voice reproved,
That I with stern delights should e'er have been so moved.

86

It is the hush of night, and all between   190
Thy margin and the mountains, dusk, yet clear,
Mellowed and mingling, yet distinctly seen,
Save darken'd Jura, whose capt heights appear
Precipitously steep; and drawing near,
There breathes a living fragrance from the shore,
Of flowers yet fresh with childhood; on the ear
Drops the light drip of the suspended oar,
Or chirps the grasshopper one good-night carol more;

87

He is an evening reveller, who makes
His life an infancy, and sings his fill;   200
At intervals, some bird from out the brakes,
Starts into voice a moment, then is still.
There seems a floating whisper on the hill,
But that is fancy, for the starlight dews
All silently their tears of love instil,
Weeping themselves away, till they infuse
Deep into Nature's breast the spirit of her hues.

88

Ye stars! which are the poetry of heaven!
If in your bright leaves we would read the fate
Of men and empires,—'tis to be forgiven,   210
That in our aspirations to be great,
Our destinies o'erleap their mortal state,

And claim a kindred with you; for ye are
A beauty and a mystery, and create
In us such love and reverence from afar,
That fortune, fame, power, life, have named themselves a star.

89

All heaven and earth are still—though not in sleep,
But breathless, as we grow when feeling most;
And silent, as we stand in thoughts too deep:—
All heaven and earth are still: From the high host   220
Of stars, to the lull'd lake and mountain-coast,
All is concentred in a life intense,
Where not a beam, nor air, nor leaf is lost,
But hath a part of being, and a sense
Of that which is of all Creator and defence.

90

Then stirs the feeling infinite, so felt
In solitude, where we are *least* alone;
A truth, which through our being then doth melt
And purifies from self: it is a tone,
The soul and source of music, which makes known   230
Eternal harmony, and sheds a charm,
Like to the fabled Cytherea's zone,
Binding all things with beauty;—'twould disarm
The spectre Death, had he substantial power to harm.

91

Not vainly did the early Persian make
His altar the high places and the peak
Or earth-o'ergazing mountains, and thus take
A fit and unwall'd temple, there to seek
The Spirit, in whose honour shrines are weak,
Uprear'd of human hands. Come, and compare   240
Columns and idol-dwellings, Goth or Greek,
With Nature's realms of worship, earth and air,
Nor fix on fond abodes to circumscribe thy prayer!

92

The sky is changed!—and such a change! Oh night,
And storm, and darkness, ye are wondrous strong,
Yet lovely in your strength, as is the light
Of a dark eye in woman! Far along,
From peak to peak, the rattling crags among
Leaps the live thunder! Not from one lone cloud,
But every mountain now hath found a tongue,   250
And Jura answers, through her misty shroud,
Back to the joyous Alps, who call to her aloud!

93

And this is in the night:—Most glorious night!
Thou wert not sent for slumber! let me be
A sharer in thy fierce and far delight,—
A portion of the tempest and of thee!
How the lit lake shines, a phosphoric sea,
And the big rain comes dancing to the earth!
And now again 'tis black,—and now, the glee
Of the loud hills shakes with its mountain-mirth,   260
As if they did rejoice o'er a young earthquake's birth.

94

Now, where the swift Rhone cleaves his way between
Heights which appear as lovers who have parted
In hate, whose mining depths so intervene,
That they can meet no more, though broken-hearted;
Though in their souls, which thus each other thwarted,
Love was the very root of the fond rage
Which blighted their life's bloom, and then departed:—
Itself expired, but leaving them an age
Of years all winters,—war within themselves to wage.   270

95

Now, where the quick Rhone thus hath cleft his way,
The mightiest of the storms hath ta'en his stand:
For here, not one, but many, make their play,
And fling their thunder-bolts from hand to hand,
Flashing and cast around: of all the band,

The brightest through these parted hills hath fork'd
His lightnings,—as if he did understand,
That in such gaps as desolation work'd,
There the hot shaft should blast whatever therein lurk'd.

96

Sky, mountains, river, winds, lake, lightnings! ye!   280
With night, and clouds, and thunder, and a soul
To make these felt and feeling, well may be
Things that have made me watchful; the far roll
Of your departing voices, is the knoll
Of what in me is sleepless,—if I rest.
But where of ye, oh tempests! is the goal?
Are ye like those within the human breast?
Or do ye find, at length, like eagles, some high nest?

97

Could I embody and unbosom now
That which is most within me,—could I wreak   290
My thoughts upon expression, and thus throw
Soul, heart, mind, passions, feelings, strong or weak,
All that I would have sought, and all I seek,
Bear, know, feel, and yet breathe—into *one* word,
And that one word were Lightning, I would speak;
But as it is, I live and die unheard,
With a most voiceless thought, sheathing it as a sword.

from *MANFRED*

A Dramatic Poem

There are more things in heaven and earth, Horatio,
Than are dreamt of in your philosophy.

*The Scene of the Drama is amongst the Higher Alps—partly in
the Castle of Manfred, and partly in the Mountains.*

Act I

SCENE I

MANFRED *alone—Scene, a Gothic gallery—Time, Midnight.*

MAN. The lamp must be replenish'd, but even then
   It will not burn so long as I must watch:
   My slumbers—if I slumber—are not sleep,
   But a continuance of enduring thought,
   Which then I can resist not: in my heart
   There is a vigil, and these eyes but close
   To look within; and yet I live, and bear
   The aspect and the form of breathing men.
   But grief should be the instructor of the wise;
   Sorrow is knowledge: they who know the most   10
   Must mourn the deepest o'er the fatal truth,
   The Tree of Knowledge is not that of Life.
   Philosophy and science, and the springs
   Of wonder, and the wisdom of the world,
   I have essayed, and in my mind there is
   A power to make these subject to itself—
   But they avail not: I have done men good,
   And I have met with good even among men—
   But this avail'd not: I have had my foes,
   And none have baffled, many fallen before me—   20
   But this avail'd not:—Good, or evil, life,
   Powers, passions, all I see in other beings,
   Have been to me as rain unto the sands,
   Since that all-nameless hour. I have no dread,
   And feel the curse to have no natural fear,
   Nor fluttering throb, that beats with hopes or wishes,

Or lurking love of something on the earth.—
Now to my task.—
           Mysterious Agency!
Ye spirits of the unbounded Universe.
Whom I have sought in darkness and in light—   30
Ye, who do compass earth about, and dwell
In subtler essence—ye, to whom the tops
Of mountains inaccessible are haunts,
And earth's and ocean's caves familiar things—
I call upon ye by the written charm
Which gives me power upon you——Rise! appear!
                            [*A pause*]
They come not yet.—Now by the voice of him
Who is the first among you—by this sign,
Which makes you tremble—by the claims of him
Who is undying,—Rise! appear!——Appear![*A pause*] 40
If it be so.—Spirits of earth and air,
Ye shall not thus elude me: by a power,
Deeper than all yet urged, a tyrant-spell,
Which had its birth-place in a star condemn'd,
The burning wreck of a demolish'd world,
A wandering hell in the eternal space;
By the strong curse which is upon my soul,
The thought which is within me and around me,
I do compel ye to my will.—Appear!
   [*A star is seen at the darker end of the gallery; it is stationary;
     and a voice is heard singing*]

FIRST SPIRIT.

Mortal! to thy bidding bow'd,   50
From my mansion in the cloud,
Which the breath of twilight builds,
And the summer's sun-set gilds
With the azure and vermilion,
Which is mix'd for my pavilion;
Though thy quest may be forbidden,
On a star-beam I have ridden;
To thine adjuration bow'd,
Mortal—be thy wish avow'd!

Voice of the SECOND SPIRIT.

Mont Blanc is the monarch of mountains,   60
   They crowned him long ago
On a throne of rocks, in a robe of clouds,
   With a diadem of snow.
Around his waist are forests braced,
   The Avalanche in his hand;
But ere it fall, that thundering ball
   Must pause for my command.
The Glacier's cold and restless mass
   Moves onward day by day;
But I am he who bids it pass,   70
   Or with its ice delay.
I am the spirit of the place,
   Could make the mountain bow
And quiver to his cavern'd base—
   And what with me wouldst *Thou*?

Voice of the THIRD SPIRIT.

In the blue depth of the waters,
   Where the wave hath no strife,
Where the wind is a stranger,
   And the sea-snake hath life,
Where the Mermaid is decking   80
   Her green hair with shells;
Like the storm on the surface
   Came the sound of thy spells;
O'er my calm Hall of Coral
   The deep echo roll'd—
To the Spirit of Ocean
   Thy wishes unfold!

FOURTH SPIRIT.

Where the slumbering earthquake
   Lies pillow'd on fire,
And the lakes of bitumen   90
   Rise boilingly higher;
Where the roots of the Andes
   Strike deep in the earth,
As their summits to heaven
   Shoot soaringly forth;

I have quitted my birth-place,
  Thy bidding to bide—
Thy spell hath subdued me,
  Thy will be my guide!

FIFTH SPIRIT.

I am the Rider of the wind,   100
  The Stirrer of the storm;
The hurricane I left behind
  Is yet with lightning warm;
To speed to thee, o'er shore and sea
  I swept upon the blast:
The fleet I met sailed well, and yet
  'Twill sink ere night be past.

SIXTH SPIRIT.

My dwelling is the shadow of the night,
Why doth thy magic torture me with light?

SEVENTH SPIRIT.

The star which rules thy destiny,   110
Was ruled, ere earth began, by me:
It was a world as fresh and fair
As e'er revolved round sun in air;
Its course was free and regular,
Space bosom'd not a lovelier star.
The hour arrived—and it became
A wandering mass of shapeless flame,
A pathless comet, and a curse,
The menace of the universe;
Still rolling on with innate force,   120
Without a sphere, without a course,
A bright deformity on high,
The monster of the upper sky!
And thou! beneath its influence born—
Thou worm! whom I obey and scorn—
Forced by a power (which is not thine,
And lent thee but to make thee mine)
For this brief moment to descend,
Where these weak spirits round thee bend
And parley with a thing like thee—   130
What wouldst thou, Child of clay! with me?

The SEVEN SPIRITS.

Earth, ocean, air, night, mountains, winds, thy star,
    Are at thy beck and bidding, Child of Clay!
Before thee at thy quest their spirits are—
    What wouldst thou with us, son of mortals—say?

MAN. Forgetfulness——
FIRST SPIRIT.   Of what—of whom—and why?
MAN. Of that which is within me; read it there—
  Ye know it, and I cannot utter it.
SPIRIT. We can but give thee that which we possess:
  Ask of us subjects, sovereignty, the power   140
  O'er earth, the whole, or portion, or a sign
  Which shall control the elements, whereof
  We are the dominators, each and all,
  These shall be thine.
MAN.   Oblivion, self-oblivion—
  Can ye not wring from out the hidden realms
  Ye offer so profusely what I ask?
SPIRIT. It is not in our essence, in our skill;
  But—thou mayst die.
MAN.   Will death bestow it on me?
SPIRIT. We are immortal, and do not forget;
  We are eternal; and to us the past   150
  Is, as the future, present. Art thou answered?
MAN. Ye mock me—but the power which brought ye here
  Hath made you mine. Slaves, scoff not at my will!
  The mind, the spirit, the Promethean spark,
  The lightning of my being, is as bright,
  Pervading, and far-darting as your own,
  And shall not yield to yours, though coop'd in clay!
  Answer, or I will teach ye what I am.
SPIRIT. We answer as we answered; our reply
  Is even in thine own words.
MAN.   Why say ye so?   160
SPIRIT. If, as thou say'st, thine essence be as ours,
  We have replied in telling thee, the thing
  Mortals call death hath nought to do with us.
MAN. I then have call'd ye from your realms in vain;
  Ye cannot, or ye will not, aid me.
SPIRIT.   Say;

What we possess we offer; it is thine:
Bethink ere thou dismiss us, ask again—
Kingdom, and sway, and strength, and length of days——
MAN. Accursed! what have I to do with days?
They are too long already.—Hence—begone!   170
SPIRIT. Yet pause: being here, our will would do thee service;
Bethink thee, is there then no other gift
Which we can make not worthless in thine eyes?
MAN. No, none: yet stay—one moment, ere we part—
I would behold ye face to face. I hear
Your voices, sweet and melancholy sounds,
As music on the waters; and I see
The steady aspect of a clear large star;
But nothing more. Approach me as ye are,
Or one, or all, in your accustom'd forms.   180
SPIRIT. We have no forms beyond the elements
Of which we are the mind and principle:
But choose a form—in that we will appear.
MAN. I have no choice; there is no form on earth
Hideous or beautiful to me. Let him,
Who is most powerful of ye, take such aspect
As unto him may seem most fitting.—Come!
SEVENTH SPIRIT [*Appearing in the shape of a beautiful female
      figure*]. Behold!
MAN.   Oh God! if it be thus, and *thou*
Art not a madness and a mockery,
I yet might be most happy.—I will clasp thee,   190
And we again will be——   [*The figure vanishes*
                  My heart is crush'd!
                        [MANFRED *falls senseless*
   [*A voice is heard in the Incantation which follows*]

         When the moon is on the wave,
            And the glow-worm in the grass,
         And the meteor on the grave,
            And the wisp on the morass;
         When the falling stars are shooting,
         And the answer'd owls are hooting,
         And the silent leaves are still
         In the shadow of the hill,

Shall my soul be upon thine,   200
With a power and with a sign.

Though thy slumber may be deep,
Yet thy spirit shall not sleep,
There are shades which will not vanish,
There are thoughts thou canst not banish;
By a power to thee unknown,
Thou canst never be alone;
Thou art wrapt as with a shroud,
Thou art gathered in a cloud;
And for ever shalt thou dwell   210
In the spirit of this spell.

Though thou seest me not pass by,
Thou shalt feel me with thine eye
As a thing that, though unseen,
Must be near thee, and hath been;
And when in that secret dread
Thou hast turn'd around thy head,
Thou shalt marvel I am not
As thy shadow on the spot,
And the power which thou dost feel   220
Shall be what thou must conceal.

And a magic voice and verse
Hath baptized thee with a curse;
And a spirit of the air
Hath begirt thee with a snare;
In the wind there is a voice
Shall forbid thee to rejoice;
And to thee shall Night deny
All the quiet of her sky;
And the day shall have a sun,   230
Which shall make thee wish it done.

From thy false tears I did distil
An essence which hath strength to kill;
From thy own heart I then did wring
The black blood in its blackest spring;
From thy own smile I snatch'd the snake,

For there it coil'd as in a brake;
From thy own lip I drew the charm
Which gave all these their chiefest harm;
In proving every poison known,   240
I found the strongest was thine own.

By thy cold breast and serpent smile,
By thy unfathom'd gulfs of guile,
By that most seeming virtuous eye,
By thy shut soul's hypocrisy;
By the perfection of thine art
Which pass'd for human thine own heart;
By thy delight in others' pain,
And by thy brotherhood of Cain,
I call upon thee! and compel   250
Thyself to be thy proper Hell!

And on thy head I pour the vial
Which doth devote thee to this trial;
Nor to slumber, nor to die,
Shall be in thy destiny;
Though thy death shall still seem near
To thy wish, but as a fear;
Lo! the spell now works around thee,
And the clankless chain hath bound thee;
O'er thy heart and brain together   260
Hath the word been pass'd—now wither!

[*So, We'll Go No More a Roving*]

1

So, we'll go no more a roving
   So late into the night,
Though the heart be still as loving,
   And the moon be still as bright.

2

For the sword outwears its sheath,
   And the soul wears out the breast,
And the heart must pause to breathe,
   And love itself have rest.

3

Though the night was made for loving,
   And the day returns too soon,   10
Yet we'll go no more a roving
   By the light of the moon.

                   [1817]

from *BEPPO*

A Venetian Story

ROSALIND. Farewell, Monsieur Traveller: Look you lisp, and wear strange suits; disable all the benefits of your own country; be out of love with your Nativity, and almost chide God for making you that countenance you are; or I will scarce think that you have swam in a GONDOLA.

AS YOU LIKE IT, IV. i

          Annotation of the Commentators.
   That is, been at *Venice*, which was much visited by the young English gentlemen of those times, and was then what *Paris* is *now*—the seat of all dissoluteness. S.A.

1

'Tis known, at least it should be, that throughout
   All countries of the Catholic persuasion,
Some weeks before Shrove Tuesday comes about,
   The people take their fill of recreation,
And buy repentance, ere they grow devout,
   However high their rank, or low their station,
With fiddling, feasting, dancing, drinking, masquing,
And other things which may be had for asking.

2

The moment night with dusky mantle covers
   The skies (and the more duskily the better),   10
The time less liked by husbands than by lovers
   Begins, and prudery flings aside her fetter;
And gaiety on restless tiptoe hovers,
   Giggling with all the gallants who beset her;
And there are songs and quavers, roaring, humming,
Guitars, and every other sort of strumming.

3

And there are dresses splendid, but fantastical,
   Masks of all times and nations, Turks and Jews,
And harlequins and clowns, with feats gymnastical,
   Greeks, Romans, Yankee-doodles, and Hindoos;   20
All kinds of dress, except the ecclesiastical,
   All people, as their fancies hit, may choose,
But no one in these parts may quiz the clergy,
Therefore take heed, ye Freethinkers! I charge ye.

4

You'd better walk about begirt with briars,
   Instead of coat and smallclothes, than put on
A single stitch reflecting upon friars,
   Although you swore it only was in fun;
They'd haul you o'er the coals, and stir the fires
   Of Phlegethon with every mother's son,   30
Nor say one mass to cool the cauldron's bubble
That boiled your bones, unless you paid them double.

5

But saving this, you may put on whate'er
   You like by way of doublet, cape, or cloak,
Such as in Monmouth-street, or in Rag Fair,
   Would rig you out in seriousness or joke;
And even in Italy such places are
   With prettier names in softer accents spoke,
For, bating Covent Garden, I can hit on
No place that's called 'Piazza' in Great Britain.   40

6

This feast is named the Carnival, which being
   Interpreted, implies 'farewell to flesh':
So call'd, because the name and thing agreeing,
   Through Lent they live on fish both salt and fresh.
But why they usher Lent with so much glee in,
   Is more than I can tell, although I guess
'Tis as we take a glass with friends at parting,
In the stage-coach or packet, just at starting.

7

And thus they bid farewell to carnal dishes,
   And solid meats, and highly spic'd ragouts,   50
To live for forty days on ill-dress'd fishes,
   Because they have no sauces to their stews,
A thing which causes many 'poohs' and 'pishes',
   And several oaths (which would not suit the Muse),
From travellers accustom'd from a boy
To eat their salmon, at the least, with soy;

8

And therefore humbly I would recommend
   'The curious in fish-sauce', before they cross
The sea, to bid their cook, or wife, or friend,
   Walk or ride to the Strand, and buy in gross   60
(Or if set out beforehand, these may send
   By any means least liable to loss),
Ketchup, Soy, Chili-vinegar, and Harvey,
Or, by the Lord! a Lent will well nigh starve ye;

9

That is to say, if your religion's Roman,
   And you at Rome would do as Romans do,
According to the proverb,—although no man,
   If foreign, is oblig'd to fast; and you,
If protestant, or sickly, or a woman,
   Would rather dine in sin on a ragout—   70
Dine, and be d—d! I don't mean to be coarse,
But that's the penalty, to say no worse.

10

Of all the places where the Carnival
   Was most facetious in the days of yore,
For dance, and song, and serenade, and ball,
   And masque, and mime, and mystery, and more
Than I have time to tell now, or at all,
   Venice the bell from every city bore,
And at the moment when I fix my story,
That sea-born city was in all her glory.   80

11

They've pretty faces yet, those same Venetians,
   Black eyes, arch'd brows, and sweet expressions still,
Such as of old were copied from the Grecians,
   In ancient arts by moderns mimick'd ill;
And like so many Venuses of Titian's
   (The best's at Florence—see it, if ye will)
They look when leaning over the balcony,
Or stepp'd from out a picture by Giorgione,

12

Whose tints are truth and beauty at their best;
   And when you to Manfrini's palace go,   90
That picture (howsoever fine the rest)
   Is loveliest to my mind of all the show;
It may perhaps be also to *your* zest,
   And that's the cause I rhyme upon it so,
'Tis but a portrait of his son, and wife,
And self; but *such* a woman! love in life!

13

Love in full life and length, not love ideal,
   No, nor ideal beauty, that fine name,
But something better still, so very real,
   That the sweet model must have been the same;   100
A thing that you would purchase, beg, or steal,
   Wer't not impossible, besides a shame:
The face recalls some face, as 'twere with pain,
You once have seen, but ne'er will see again;

14

One of those forms which flit by us, when we
   Are young, and fix our eyes on every face;
And, oh! the loveliness at times we see
   In momentary gliding, the soft grace,
The youth, the bloom, the beauty which agree,
   In many a nameless being we retrace,   110
Whose course and home we knew not, nor shall know,
Like the lost Pleiad seen no more below.

.   .   .   .

41

With all its sinful doings, I must say,
   That Italy's a pleasant place to me,
Who love to see the Sun shine every day,
   And vines (not nail'd to walls) from tree to tree
Festoon'd, much like the back scene of a play,
   Or melodrame, which people flock to see,
When the first act is ended by a dance
In vineyards copied from the south of France.   120

42

I like on Autumn evenings to ride out,
   Without being forc'd to bid my groom be sure
My cloak is round his middle strapp'd about,
   Because the skies are not the most secure;
I know too that, if stopp'd upon my route,
   Where the green alleys windingly allure,
Reeling with *grapes* red waggons choke the way,—
In England 'twould be dung, dust, or a dray.

43

I also like to dine on becaficas,
   To see the Sun set, sure he'll rise to-morrow,   130
Not through a misty morning twinkling weak as
   A drunken man's dead eye in maudlin sorrow,
But with all Heaven t' himself; that day will break as
   Beauteous as cloudless, nor be forc'd to borrow
That sort of farthing candlelight which glimmers
Where reeking London's smoky cauldron simmers.

44

I love the language, that soft bastard Latin,
   Which melts like kisses from a female mouth,
And sounds as if it should be writ on satin,
   With syllables which breathe of the sweet South,   140
And gentle liquids gliding all so pat in,
   That not a single accent seems uncouth,
Like our harsh northern whistling, grunting guttural,
Which we're oblig'd to hiss, and spit, and sputter all.

45

I like the women too (forgive my folly),
   From the rich peasant-cheek of ruddy bronze,
And large black eyes that flash on you a volley
   Of rays that say a thousand things at once,
To the high dama's brow, more melancholy,
   But clear, and with a wild and liquid glance,   150
Heart on her lips, and soul within her eyes,
Soft as her clime, and sunny as her skies.

46

Eve of the land which still is Paradise!
   Italian beauty! didst thou not inspire
Raphael, who died in thy embrace, and vies
   With all we know of Heaven, or can desire,
In what he hath bequeath'd us?—in what guise,
   Though flashing from the fervour of the lyre,
Would *words* describe thy past and present glow,
While yet Canova can create below?   160

47

'England! with all thy faults I love thee still,'
 I said at Calais, and have not forgot it;
I like to speak and lucubrate my fill;
 I like the government (but that is not it);
I like the freedom of the press and quill;
 I like the Habeas Corpus (when we've got it);
I like a parliamentary debate,
Particularly when 'tis not too late;

48

I like the taxes, when they're not too many;
 I like a seacoal fire, when not too dear;   170
I like a beef-steak, too, as well as any;
 Have no objection to a pot of beer;
I like the weather, when it is not rainy,
 That is, I like two months of every year.
And so God save the Regent, Church, and King!
Which means that I like all and every thing.

49

Our standing army, and disbanded seamen,
 Poor's rate, Reform, my own, the nation's debt,
Our little riots just to show we are free men,
 Our trifling bankruptcies in the Gazette,   180
Our cloudy climate, and our chilly women,
 All these I can forgive, and those forget,
And greatly venerate our recent glories,
And wish they were not owing to the Tories.

50

But to my tale of Laura,—for I find
 Digression is a sin, that by degrees
Becomes exceeding tedious to my mind,
 And, therefore, may the reader too displease—
The gentle reader, who may wax unkind,
 And caring little for the author's ease,   190
Insist on knowing what he means, a hard
And hapless situation for a bard.

51

Oh that I had the art of easy writing
   What should be easy reading! could I scale
Parnassus, where the Muses sit inditing
   Those pretty poems never known to fail,
How quickly would I print (the world delighting)
   A Grecian, Syrian, or *Ass*yrian tale;
And sell you, mix'd with western sentimentalism,
Some samples of the finest Orientalism.   200

52

But I am but a nameless sort of person
   (A broken Dandy lately on my travels)
And take for rhyme, to hook my rambling verse on,
   The first that Walker's Lexicon unravels,
And when I can't find that, I put a worse on,
   Not caring as I ought for critics' cavils;
I've half a mind to tumble down to prose,
But verse is more in fashion—so here goes!

[1818]

from CHILDE HAROLD'S PILGRIMAGE.
CANTO IV

1

I stood in Venice, on the Bridge of Sighs;
A palace and a prison on each hand:
I saw from out the wave her structures rise
As from the stroke of the enchanter's wand:
A thousand years their cloudy wings expand
Around me, and a dying Glory smiles
O'er the far times, when many a subject land
Look'd to the winged Lion's marble piles,
Where Venice sate in state, thron'd on her hundred isles!

2

She looks a sea Cybele, fresh from ocean,   10
Rising with her tiara of proud towers
At airy distance, with majestic motion,
A ruler of the waters and their powers:
And such she was;—her daughters had their dowers
From spoils of nations, and the exhaustless East
Pour'd in her lap all gems in sparkling showers.
In purple was she robed, and of her feast
Monarchs partook, and deem'd their dignity increas'd.

3

In Venice Tasso's echoes are no more,
And silent rows the songless gondolier;   20
Her palaces are crumbling to the shore,
And music meets not always now the ear:
Those days are gone—but Beauty still is here.
States fall, arts fade—but Nature doth not die,
Nor yet forget how Venice once was dear,
The pleasant place of all festivity,
The revel of the earth, the masque of Italy!

4

But unto us she hath a spell beyond
Her name in story, and her long array

Of mighty shadows, whose dim forms despond   30
Above the dogeless city's vanish'd sway;
Ours is a trophy which will not decay
With the Rialto; Shylock and the Moor,
And Pierre, can not be swept or worn away—
The keystones of the arch! though all were o'er,
For us repeopled were the solitary shore.

5

The beings of the mind are not of clay;
Essentially immortal, they create
And multiply in us a brighter ray
And more beloved existence: that which Fate   40
Prohibits to dull life, in this our state
Of mortal bondage, by these spirits supplied
First exiles, then replaces what we hate;
Watering the heart whose early flowers have died,
And with a fresher growth replenishing the void.

6

Such is the refuge of our youth and age,
The first from Hope, the last from Vacancy;
And this worn feeling peoples many a page;
And, may be, that which grows beneath mine eye:
Yet there are things whose strong reality   50
Outshines our fairy-land; in shape and hues
More beautiful than our fantastic sky,
And the strange constellations which the Muse
O'er her wild universe is skilful to diffuse:

7

I saw or dreamed of such,—but let them go—
They came like truth, and disappeared like dreams;
And whatsoe'er they were—are now but so:
I could replace them if I would, still teems
My mind with many a form which aptly seems
Such as I sought for, and at moments found;   60
Let these too go—for waking Reason deems
Such over-weening phantasies unsound,
And other voices speak, and other sights surround.

·   ·   ·   ·

93

What from this barren being do we reap?
Our senses narrow, and our reason frail,
Life short, and truth a gem which loves the deep,
And all things weigh'd in custom's falsest scale;
Opinion an omnipotence,—whose veil
Mantles the earth with darkness, until right
And wrong are accidents, and men grow pale   70
Lest their own judgments should become too bright,
And their free thoughts be crimes, and earth have too much light.

94

And thus they plod in sluggish misery,
Rotting from sire to son, and age to age,
Proud of their trampled nature, and so die,
Bequeathing their hereditary rage
To the new race of inborn slaves, who wage
War for their chains, and rather than be free,
Bleed gladiator-like, and still engage
Within the same arena where they see   80
Their fellows fall before, like leaves of the same tree.

95

I speak not of men's creeds—they rest between
Man and his Maker—but of things allowed,
Averr'd, and known,—and daily, hourly seen—
The yoke that is upon us doubly bowed,
And the intent of tyranny avowed,
The edict of Earth's rulers, who are grown
The apes of him who humbled once the proud,
And shook them from their slumbers on the throne;
Too glorious, were this all his mighty arm had done.   90

96

Can tyrants but by tyrants conquered be,
And Freedom find no champion and no child
Such as Columbia saw arise when she
Sprung forth a Pallas, armed and undefiled?
Or must such minds be nourished in the wild,

Deep in the unpruned forest, 'midst the roar
Of cataracts, where nursing Nature smiled
On infant Washington? Has Earth no more
Such seeds within her breast, or Europe no such shore?

97

But France got drunk with blood to vomit crime, 100
And fatal have her Saturnalia been
To Freedom's cause, in every age and clime;
Because the deadly days which we have seen,
And vile Ambition, that built up between
Man and his hopes an adamantine wall,
And the base pageant last upon the scene,
Are grown the pretext for the eternal thrall
Which nips life's tree, and dooms man's worst, his second fall.

98

Yet, Freedom! yet thy banner, torn, but flying,
Streams like the thunder-storm *against* the wind; 110
Thy trumpet voice, though broken now and dying,
The loudest still the tempest leaves behind;
Thy tree hath lost its blossoms, and the rind,
Chopp'd by the axe, looks rough and little worth,
But the sap lasts,—and still the seed we find
Sown deep, even in the bosom of the North;
So shall a better spring less bitter fruit bring forth.

99

There is a stern round tower of other days,
Firm as a fortress, with its fence of stone,
Such as an army's baffled strength delays, 120
Standing with half its battlements alone,
And with two thousand years of ivy grown,
The garland of eternity, where wave
The green leaves over all by time o'erthrown;—
What was this tower of strength? within its cave
What treasure lay so lock'd, so hid?—A woman's grave.

100

But who was she, the lady of the dead,
Tombed in a palace? Was she chaste and fair?
Worthy a king's—or more—a Roman's bed?
What race of chiefs and heroes did she bear?   130
What daughter of her beauties was the heir?
How lived—how loved—how died she? Was she not
So honoured—and conspicuously there,
Where meaner relics must not dare to rot,
Placed to commemorate a more than mortal lot?

101

Was she as those who love their lords, or they
Who love the lords of others? such have been,
Even in the olden time Rome's annals say.
Was she a matron of Cornelia's mien,
Or the light air of Egypt's graceful queen,   140
Profuse of joy—or 'gainst it did she war,
Inveterate in virtue? Did she lean
To the soft side of the heart, or wisely bar
Love from amongst her griefs?—for such the affections are.

102

Perchance she died in youth: it may be, bowed
With woes far heavier than the ponderous tomb
That weighed upon her gentle dust, a cloud
Might gather o'er her beauty, and a gloom
In her dark eye, prophetic of the doom
Heaven gives its favourites—early death; yet shed   150
A sunset charm around her, and illume
With hectic light, the Hesperus of the dead,
Of her consuming cheek the autumnal leaf-like red.

103

Perchance she died in age—surviving all,
Charms, kindred, children—with the silver grey
On her long tresses, which might yet recall,
It may be, still a something of the day
When they were braided, and her proud array

And lovely form were envied, praised, and eyed
By Rome—But whither would Conjecture stray? 160
Thus much alone we know—Metella died,
The wealthiest Roman's wife; Behold his love or pride!

104

I know not why—but standing thus by thee
It seems as if I had thine inmate known,
Thou tomb! and other days come back on me
With recollected music, though the tone
Is changed and solemn, like the cloudy groan
Of dying thunder on the distant wind;
Yet could I seat me by this ivied stone
Till I had bodied forth the heated mind 170
Forms from the floating wreck which Ruin leaves behind;

105

And from the planks, far shattered o'er the rocks,
Built me a little bark of hope, once more
To battle with the ocean and the shocks
Of the loud breakers, and the ceaseless roar
Which rushes on the solitary shore
Where all lies foundered that was ever dear:
But could I gather from the wave-worn store
Enough for my rude boat, where should I steer?
There woos no home, nor hope, nor life, save what is here. 180

106

Then let the winds howl on! their harmony
Shall henceforth be my music, and the night
The sound shall temper with the owlet's cry,
As I now hear them, in the fading light
Dim o'er the bird of darkness' native site,
Answering each other on the Palatine,
With their large eyes, all glistening grey and bright,
And sailing pinions.—Upon such a shrine
What are our petty griefs?—let me not number mine.

107

Cypress and ivy, weed and wallflower grown   190
Matted and mass'd together, hillocks heap'd
On what were chambers, arch crush'd, column strown
In fragments, chok'd up vaults, and frescos steep'd
In subterranean damps, where the owl peep'd,
Deeming it midnight:—Temples, baths, or halls?
Pronounce who can; for all that Learning reap'd
From her research hath been, that these are walls—
Behold the Imperial Mount! 'tis thus the mighty falls.

108

There is the moral of all human tales;
'Tis but the same rehearsal of the past,   200
First Freedom, and then Glory—when that fails,
Wealth, vice, corruption,—barbarism at last.
And History, with all her volumes vast,
Hath but *one* page,—'tis better written here,
Where gorgeous Tyranny had thus amass'd
All treasures, all delights, that eye or ear,
Heart, soul could seek, tongue ask—Away with words! draw near,

109

Admire, exult—despise—laugh, weep,—for here
There is such matter for all feeling:—Man!
Thou pendulum betwixt a smile and tear,   210
Ages and realms are crowded in this span,
This mountain, whose obliterated plan
The pyramid of empires pinnacled,
Of Glory's gewgaws shining in the van
Till the sun's rays with added flame were fill'd!
Where are its golden roofs? where those who dared to build?

.   .   .   .   .   .

115

Egeria! sweet creation of some heart
Which found no mortal resting-place so fair
As thine ideal breast; whate'er thou art
Or wert,—a young Aurora of the air,   220

The nympholepsy of some fond despair;
Or, it might be, a beauty of the earth,
Who found a more than common votary there
Too much adoring; whatso'er thy birth,
Thou wert a beautiful thought, and softly bodied forth.

116

The mosses of thy fountain still are sprinkled
With thine Elysian water-drops; the face
Of thy cave-guarded spring, with years unwrinkled,
Reflects the meek-eyed genius of the place,
Whose green, wild margin now no more erase   230
Art's works; nor must the delicate waters sleep,
Prisoned in marble, bubbling from the base
Of the cleft statue, with a gentle leap
The rill runs o'er, and round, fern, flowers, and ivy, creep,

117

Fantastically tangled; the green hills
Are clothed with early blossoms, through the grass
The quick-eyed lizard rustles, and the bills
Of summer-birds sing welcome as ye pass;
Flowers fresh in hue, and many in their class,
Implore the pausing step, and with their dyes   240
Dance in the soft breeze in a fairy mass;
The sweetness of the violet's deep blue eyes,
Kiss'd by the breath of heaven, seems coloured by its skies.

118

Here didst thou dwell, in this enchanted cover,
Egeria! thy all heavenly bosom beating
For the far footsteps of thy mortal lover;
The purple Midnight veil'd that mystic meeting
With her most starry canopy, and seating
Thyself by thine adorer, what befell?
This cave was surely shaped out for the greeting   250
Of an enamour'd Goddess, and the cell
Haunted by holy Love—the earliest oracle!

119

And didst thou not, thy breast to his replying,
Blend a celestial with a human heart;
And Love, which dies as it was born, in sighing,
Share with immortal transports? could thine art
Make them indeed immortal, and impart
The purity of heaven to earthly joys,
Expel the venom and not blunt the dart—
The dull satiety which all destroys—   260
And root from out the soul the deadly weed which cloys?

120

Alas! Our young affections run to waste,
Or water but the desart; whence arise
But weeds of dark luxuriance, tares of haste,
Rank at the core, though tempting to the eyes,
Flowers whose wild odours breathe but agonies,
And trees whose gums are poison; such the plants
Which spring beneath her steps as Passion flies
O'er the world's wilderness, and vainly pants
For some celestial fruit forbidden to our wants.   270

121

Oh Love! no habitant of earth thou art—
An unseen seraph, we believe in thee,
A faith whose martyrs are the broken heart,
But never yet hath seen, nor e'er shall see
The naked eye, thy form, as it should be;
The mind hath made thee, as it peopled heaven,
Even with its own desiring phantasy,
And to a thought such shape and image given,
As haunts the unquench'd soul—parch'd—wearied—wrung—and
    riven.

122

Of its own beauty is the mind diseased,   280
And fevers into false creation:—where,
Where are the forms the sculptor's soul hath seized?
In him alone. Can Nature show so fair?

Where are the charms and virtues which we dare
Conceive in boyhood and pursue as men,
The unreach'd Paradise of our despair,
Which o'er-informs the pencil and the pen,
And overpowers the page where it would bloom again?

123

Who loves, raves—'tis youth's frenzy—but the cure
Is bitterer still; as charm by charm unwinds   290
Which robed our idols, and we see too sure
Nor worth nor beauty dwells from out the mind's
Ideal shape of such; yet still it binds
The fatal spell, and still it draws us on,
Reaping the whirlwind from the oft-sown winds;
The stubborn heart, its alchemy begun,
Seems ever near the prize,—wealthiest when most undone.

124

We wither from our youth, we gasp away—
Sick—sick; unfound the boon—unslaked the thirst,
Though to the last, in verge of our decay,   300
Some phantom lures, such as we sought at first—
But all too late,—so are we doubly curst.
Love, fame, ambition, avarice—'tis the same,
Each idle—and all ill—and none the worst—
For all are meteors with a different name,
And Death the sable smoke where vanishes the flame.

125

Few—none—find what they love or could have loved,
Though accident, blind contact, and the strong
Necessity of loving, have removed
Antipathies—but to recur, ere long,   310
Envenomed with irrevocable wrong;
And Circumstance, that unspiritual god
And miscreator, makes and helps along
Our coming evils with a crutch-like rod,
Whose touch turns Hope to dust,—the dust we all have trod.

126

Our life is a false nature—'tis not in
The harmony of things,—this hard decree,
This uneradicable taint of sin,
This boundless upas, this all-blasting tree,
Whose root is earth, whose leaves and branches be   320
The skies which rain their plagues on men like dew—
Disease, death, bondage—all the woes we see—
And worse, the woes we see not—which throb through
The immedicable soul, with heart-aches ever new.

127

Yet let us ponder boldly—'tis a base
Abandonment of reason to resign
Our right of thought—our last and only place
Of refuge; this, at least, shall still be mine:
Though from our birth the faculty divine
Is chain'd and tortured—cabin'd, cribb'd, confined,   330
And bred in darkness, lest the truth should shine
Too brightly on the unprepared mind,
The beam pours in, for time and skill will couch the blind.

128

Arches on arches! as it were that Rome,
Collecting the chief trophies of her line,
Would build up all her triumphs in one dome,
Her Coliseum stands; the moonbeams shine
As 'twere its natural torches, for divine
Should be the light which streams here, to illume
This long-explored but still exhaustless mine   340
Of contemplation; and the azure gloom
Of an Italian night, where the deep skies assume

129

Hues which have words, and speak to ye of heaven,
Floats o'er this vast and wondrous monument,
And shadows forth its glory. There is given
Unto the things of earth, which time hath bent,
A spirit's feeling, and where he hath leant

His hand, but broke his scythe, there is a power
And magic in the ruined battlement,
For which the palace of the present hour   350
Must yield its pomp, and wait till ages are its dower.

130

Oh Time! the beautifier of the dead,
Adorner of the ruin, comforter
And only healer when the heart hath bled—
Time! the corrector where our judgments err,
The test of truth, love,—sole philosopher,
For all beside are sophists, from thy thrift,
Which never loses though it doth defer—
Time, the avenger! unto thee I lift
My hands, and eyes, and heart, and crave of thee a gift: 360

131

Amidst this wreck, where thou hast made a shrine
And temple more divinely desolate,
Among thy mightier offerings here are mine,
Ruins of years—though few, yet full of fate:—
If thou hast ever seen me too elate,
Hear me not; but if calmly I have borne
Good, and reserved my pride against the hate
Which shall not whelm me, let me not have worn
This iron in my soul in vain—shall *they* not mourn?

132

And thou, who never yet of human wrong   370
Left'st the unbalanced scale, great Nemesis!
Here, where the ancient paid thee homage long—
Thou, who didst call the Furies from the abyss,
And round Orestes bade them howl and hiss
For that unnatural retribution—just,
Had it but been from hands less near—in this
Thy former realm, I call thee from the dust!
Dost thou not hear my heart?—Awake! thou shalt, and must.

133

It is not that I may not have incurr'd
For my ancestral faults or mine the wound   380
I bleed withal, and, had it been conferr'd
With a just weapon, it had flowed unbound;
But now my blood shall not sink in the ground;
To thee I do devote it—*thou* shalt take
The vengeance, which shall yet be sought and found,
Which if *I* have not taken for the sake—
But let that pass—I sleep, but thou shalt yet awake.

134

And if my voice break forth, 'tis not that now
I shrink from what is suffered: let him speak
Who hath beheld decline upon my brow,   390
Or seen my mind's convulsion leave it weak;
But in this page a record will I seek.
Not in the air shall these my words disperse,
Though I be ashes; a far hour shall wreak
The deep prophetic fullness of this verse,
And pile on human heads the mountain of my curse!

135

That curse shall be Forgiveness.—Have I not—
Hear me, my mother Earth! behold it, Heaven!—
Have I not had to wrestle with my lot?
Have I not suffered things to be forgiven?   400
Have I not had my brain seared, my heart riven,
Hopes sapp'd, name blighted, Life's life lied away?
And only not to desperation driven,
Because not altogether of such clay
As rots into the souls of those whom I survey.

136

From mighty wrongs to petty perfidy
Have I not seen what human things could do?
From the loud roar of foaming calumny
To the small whisper of the as paltry few,
And subtler venom of the reptile crew,   410

The Janus glance of whose significant eye,
Learning to lie with silence, would *seem* true,
And without utterance, save the shrug or sigh,
Deal round to happy fools its speechless obloquy.

137

But I have lived, and have not lived in vain:
My mind may lose its force, my blood its fire,
And my frame perish even in conquering pain,
But there is that within me which shall tire
Torture and Time, and breathe when I expire;
Something unearthly, which they deem not of,   420
Like the remembered tone of a mute lyre,
Shall on their softened spirits sink, and move
In hearts all rocky now the late remorse of love.

138

The seal is set—Now welcome, thou dread power
Nameless, yet thus omnipotent, which here
Walk'st in the shadow of the midnight hour
With a deep awe, yet all distinct from fear;
Thy haunts are ever where the dead walls rear
Their ivy mantles, and the solemn scene
Derives from thee a sense so deep and clear   430
That we become a part of what has been,
And grow unto the spot, all-seeing but unseen.

139

And here the buzz of eager nations ran,
In murmured pity, or loud-roared applause,
As man was slaughtered by his fellow man.
And wherefore slaughtered? wherefore, but because
Such were the bloody Circus' genial laws,
And the imperial pleasure.—Wherefore not?
What matters where we fall to fill the maws
Of worms—on battle-plains or listed spot?   440
Both are but theatres where the chief actors rot.

140

I see before me the Gladiator lie:
He leans upon his hand—his manly brow
Consents to death, but conquers agony,
And his drooped head sinks gradually low—
And through his side the last drops, ebbing slow
From the red gash, fall heavy, one by one,
Like the first of a thunder-shower; and now
The arena swims around him—he is gone,
Ere ceased the inhuman shout which hail'd the wretch who
    won.   450

141

He heard it, but he heeded not—his eyes
Were with his heart, and that was far away;
He reck'd not of the life he lost nor prize,
But where his rude hut by the Danube lay
There were his young barbarians all at play,
There was their Dacian mother—he, their sire,
Butcher'd to make a Roman holiday—
All this rush'd with his blood—Shall he expire
And unavenged?—Arise! ye Goths, and glut your ire!

142

But here, where Murder breathed her bloody stream;   460
And here, where buzzing nations choked the ways,
And roar'd or murmur'd like a mountain stream
Dashing or winding as its torrent strays;
Here, where the Roman million's blame or praise
Was death or life, the playthings of a crowd,
My voice sounds much—and fall the stars' faint rays
On the arena void—seats crush'd—walls bow'd—
And galleries, where my steps seem echoes strangely loud.

143

A ruin—yet what ruin! from its mass
Walls, palaces, half-cities, have been reared;   470
Yet oft the enormous skeleton ye pass
And marvel where the spoil could have appeared,

Hath it indeed been plundered, or but cleared?
Alas! developed, opens the decay,
When the colossal fabric's form is neared:
It will not bear the brightness of the day,
Which streams too much on all years, man, have reft away.

144

But when the rising moon begins to climb
Its topmost arch, and gently pauses there;
When the stars twinkle through the loops of time,   480
And the low night-breeze waves along the air
The garland-forest, which the grey walls wear,
Like laurels on the bald first Caesar's head;
When the light shines serene but doth not glare,
Then in this magic circle raise the dead:
Heroes have trod this spot—'tis on their dust ye tread.

145

'While stands the Coliseum, Rome shall stand;
When falls the Coliseum, Rome shall fall;
And when Rome falls—the World.' From our own land
Thus spake the pilgrims o'er this mighty wall   490
In Saxon times, which we are wont to call
Ancient; and these three mortal things are still
On their foundations, and unaltered all;
Rome and her Ruin past Redemption's skill,
The World, the same wide den—of thieves, or what ye will.

.   .   .   .

155

Enter: its grandeur overwhelms thee not;
And why? it is not lessened; but thy mind,
Expanded by the genius of the spot,
Has grown colossal, and can only find
A fit abode wherein appear enshrined   500
Thy hopes of immortality; and thou
Shalt one day, if found worthy, so defined,
See thy God face to face, as thou dost now
His Holy of Holies, nor be blasted by his brow.

156

Thou movest—but increasing with the advance,
Like climbing some great Alp, which still doth rise,
Deceived by its gigantic elegance;
Vastness which grows—but grows to harmonize—
All musical in its immensities;
Rich marbles—richer painting—shrines where flame   510
The lamps of gold—and haughty dome which vies
In air with Earth's chief structures, though their frame
Sits on the firm-set ground—and this the clouds must claim.

157

Thou seest not all; but piecemeal thou must break,
To separate contemplation, the great whole;
And as the ocean many bays will make,
That ask the eye—so here condense thy soul
To more immediate objects, and control
Thy thoughts until thy mind hath got by heart
Its eloquent proportions, and unroll   520
In mighty graduations, part by part,
The glory which at once upon thee did not dart.

158

Not by its fault—but thine: Our outward sense
Is but of gradual grasp—and as it is
That what we have of feeling most intense
Outstrips our faint expression; even so this
Outshining and o'erwhelming edifice
Fools our fond gaze, and greatest of the great
Defies at first our Nature's littleness,
Till, growing with its growth, we thus dilate   530
Our spirits to the size of that they contemplate.

159

Then pause, and be enlightened; there is more
In such a survey than the sating gaze
Of wonder please, or awe which would adore
The worship of the place, or the mere praise
Of art and its great masters, who could raise

What former time, nor skill, nor thought could plan;
The fountain of sublimity displays
Its depth, and thence may draw the mind of man
Its golden sands, and learn what great conceptions can.   540

160

Or, turning to the Vatican, go see
Laocoon's torture dignifying pain—
A father's love and mortal's agony
With an immortal's patience blending:—Vain
The struggle; vain, against the coiling strain
And gripe, and deepening of the dragon's grasp,
The old man's clench; the long envenomed chain
Rivets the living links,—the enormous asp
Enforces pang on pang, and stifles gasp on gasp.

161

Or view the Lord of the unerring bow,   550
The God of life, and poesy, and light—
The Sun in human limbs arrayed, and brow
All radiant from his triumph in the fight;
The shaft hath just been shot—the arrow bright
With an immortal's vengeance; in his eye
And nostril beautiful disdain, and might,
And majesty, flash their full lightnings by,
Developing in that one glance the Deity.

162

But in his delicate form—a dream of Love,
Shaped by some solitary nymph, whose breast   560
Long'd for a deathless lover from above,
And madden'd in that vision—are exprest
All that ideal beauty ever bless'd
The mind within its inmost unearthly mood,
When each conception was a heavenly guest—
A ray of immortality—and stood,
Starlike, around, until they gathered to a god!

163

And if it be Prometheus stole from Heaven
The fire which we endure, it was repaid
By him to whom the energy was given   570
Which this poetic marble hath array'd
With an external glory—which, if made
By human hands, is not of human thought;
And Time himself hath hallowed it, nor laid
One ringlet in the dust—nor hath it caught
A tinge of years, but breathes the flame with which 'twas wrought.

.   .   .   .   .   .

179

Roll on, thou deep and dark blue ocean—roll!
Ten thousand fleets sweep over thee in vain;
Man marks the earth with ruin—his control
Stops with the shore;—upon the watery plain   580
The wrecks are all thy deed, nor doth remain
A shadow of man's ravage, save his own,
When, for a moment, like a drop of rain,
He sinks into thy depths with bubbling groan,
Without a grave, unknell'd, uncoffin'd, and unknown.

180

His steps are not upon thy paths,—thy fields
Are not a spoil for him,—thou dost arise
And shake him from thee; the vile strength he wields
For earth's destruction thou dost all despise,
Spurning him from thy bosom to the skies,   590
And send'st him, shivering in thy playful spray
And howling, to his Gods, where haply lies
His petty hope in some near port or bay,
And dashest him again to earth:—there let him lay.

181

The armaments which thunderstrike the walls
Of rock-built cities, bidding nations quake,
And monarchs tremble in their capitals,
The oak leviathans, whose huge ribs make

Their clay creator the vain title take
Of lord of thee, and arbiter of war;   600
These are thy toys, and, as the snowy flake,
They melt into thy yeast of waves, which mar
Alike the Armada's pride, or spoils of Trafalgar.

182

Thy shores are empires, changed in all save thee—
Assyria, Greece, Rome, Carthage, what are they?
Thy waters washed them power while they were free,
And many a tyrant since; their shores obey
The stranger, slave, or savage; their decay
Has dried up realms to desarts:—not so thou,
Unchangeable save to thy wild waves' play—   610
Time writes no wrinkle on thine azure brow—
Such as creation's dawn beheld, thou rollest now.

183

Thou glorious mirror, where the Almighty's form
Glasses itself in tempests; in all time,
Calm or convuls'd—in breeze, or gale, or storm,
Icing the pole, or in the torrid clime
Dark-heaving;—boundless, endless, and sublime—
The image of Eternity—the throne
Of the Invisible, even from out thy slime
The monsters of the deep are made; each zone   620
Obeys thee; thou goest forth, dread, fathomless, alone.

184

And I have loved thee, Ocean! and my joy
Of youthful sports was on thy breast to be
Borne, like thy bubbles, onward: from a boy
I wantoned with thy breakers—they to me
Were a delight; and if the freshening sea
Made them a terror—'twas a pleasing fear,
For I was as it were a child of thee,
And trusted to thy billows far and near,
And laid my hand upon thy mane—as I do here.   630

To the Po. June 2nd 1819

River! that rollest by the ancient walls
   Where dwells the Lady of my Love, when she
Walks by thy brink and there perchance recalls
   A faint and fleeting memory of me,
What if thy deep and ample stream should be
   A mirror of my heart, where she may read
The thousand thoughts I now betray to thee
   Wild as thy wave and headlong as thy speed?
What do I say? 'a mirror of my heart'?
   Are not thy waters sweeping, dark, and strong,   10
Such as my feelings were and are, thou art,
   And such as thou art were my passions long.
Time may have somewhat tamed them, not forever
   Thou overflow'st thy banks, and not for aye
The bosom overboils, congenial River!
   Thy floods subside, and mine have sunk away,
But left long wrecks behind us, yet again
   Borne on our old career unchanged we move,
Thou tendest wildly to the wilder main
   And I to loving one I should not love.   20
The current I behold will sweep beneath
   Her palace walls, and murmur at her feet,
Her eyes will look on thee, when she shall breathe
   The twilight air unchained from Summer's heat.
She will look on thee,—I have looked on thee
   Full of that thought, and from this moment ne'er
Thy waters could I name, hear named, or see
   Without the inseparable Sigh for her.
Her bright eyes will be imaged in thy Stream—
   Yes, they will meet the wave I gaze on now,   30
But mine can not even witness in a dream
   That happy wave repass me in its flow.
The wave that bears my tears returns no more
   Will She return by whom that wave shall sweep?
Both tread thy bank, both wander by thy shore,
   I near thy source, and She by the blue deep.

But that which keepeth us apart, is not
   Distance, nor depth of wave, nor space of earth,
But the distractions of a various lot,
   Ah! various as the climates of our birth!   40
A Stranger loves a lady of the land,
   Born far beyond the Mountains, but his blood
Is all meridian, as if never fanned
   By the bleak wind that chills the Polar flood.
My heart is all meridian, were it not
   I had not suffered now, nor should I be—
Despite of tortures ne'er to be forgot—
   The Slave again, Oh Love! at least of thee!
'Tis vain to struggle, I have struggled long
   To love again no more as once I loved.   50
Oh! Time! why leave this earliest Passion strong?
   To tear a heart which pants to be unmoved?

[*Stanzas*]

1

Could Love for ever
Run like a river
And Time's Endeavour
   Be tried in vain,
No other Pleasure
With this could measure
And like a Treasure
   We'd hug the chain.
But since our sighing
Ends not in dying   10
And formed for flying
   Love plumes his wing,
Then for this reason
Let's love a Season,
But let that Season be only *Spring*.—

2

When lovers parted
Feel broken-hearted,

And all hopes thwarted
  Expect to die,
A few years older   20
Ah! how much colder
They might behold her
  For whom they sigh;
When linked together
Through every weather
We pluck Love's feather
  From out his wing;
He'll sadly shiver
And droop forever
Without the plumage that sped his Spring.—   30

3

Like Chiefs of Faction
His Life is Action,
A formal paction,
  Which curbs his reign,
Obscures his Glory,
Despot no more, he
Such Territory
  Quits with disdain.
Still—still—advancing
With banners glancing
His power enhancing   40
  He must march on;
Repose but cloys him,
Retreat destroys him,
Love brooks not a degraded throne!—

4

Wait not, fond Lover!
Till years are over,
And then recover
  As from a dream.
While each bewailing
The other's failing   50
With wrath and railing
  All hideous seem;

While first decreasing
Yet not quite ceasing,
Pause not—till teazing
   All passion blight;
If once diminished
His reign is finished,
One last embrace then, and bid Good Night!   60

5

So shall Affection
To recollection
The dear connection
   Bring back with joy,
You have not waited
Till tired and hated
All passions sated
   Began to cloy.
Your last embraces
Leave no cold traces,   70
The same fond faces
   As through the past,
And Eyes the Mirrors
Of your sweet Errors
Reflect but Rapture not least though last.

6

True! Separations
Ask more than patience—
What desperations
   From such have risen!
And yet remaining,   80
What is't but chaining
Hearts, which once waning
   Beat 'gainst their prison;
Time can but cloy Love,
And Use destroy Love,
The winged Boy Love
   Is but for boys.
You'll find it torture
Though sharper, shorter,
To wean and not wear out your Joys.   90

from *DON JUAN*

Difficile est proprie communia dicere.
Hor[ace], *Epist[ola] ad Pison[es]*.

DEDICATION

1

Bob Southey! You're a poet—poet Laureate,
   And representative of all the race;
Although 'tis true you turn'd out a Tory at
   Last,—yours has lately been a common case:—
And now, my epic renegade! what are ye at,
   With all the Lakers in and out of place?
A nest of tuneful persons, to my eye
Like four and twenty blackbirds in a pie;

2

'Which pie being open'd, they began to sing'—
   (This old song and new simile holds good)   10
'A dainty dish to set before the King,'
   Or Regent, who admires such kind of food.
And Coleridge, too, has lately taken wing,
   But, like a hawk encumber'd with his hood,
Explaining metaphysics to the nation—
I wish he would explain his Explanation.

3

You, Bob! are rather insolent, you know,
   At being disappointed in your wish
To supersede all warblers here below,
   And be the only Blackbird in the dish;   20
And then you overstrain yourself, or so,
   And tumble downward like the flying fish
Gasping on deck, because you soar too high, Bob,
And fall, for lack of moisture, quite adry, Bob!

4

And Wordsworth, in a rather long 'Excursion',
   (I think the quarto holds five hundred pages)

Has given a sample from the vasty version
  Of his new system to perplex the sages:
'Tis poetry—at least by his assertion,
  And may appear so when the dogstar rages;   30
And he who understands it would be able
To add a story to the Tower of Babel.

5

You, Gentlemen! by dint of long seclusion
  From better company have kept your own
At Keswick, and through still continued fusion
  Of one another's minds at last have grown
To deem as a most logical conclusion
  That Poesy has wreaths for you alone;
There is a narrowness in such a notion
Which makes me wish you'd change your lakes for ocean. 40

6

I would not imitate the petty thought,
  Nor coin my self-love to so base a vice,
For all the glory your conversion brought,
  Since gold alone should not have been its price.
You have your salary—was't for that you wrought?
  And Wordsworth has his place in the Excise.
You're shabby fellows—true—but poets still,
And duly seated on the immortal hill.

7

Your bays may hide the baldness of your brows,
  Perhaps some virtuous blushes—let them go,   50
To you I envy neither fruit nor boughs—
  And for the fame you would engross below
The field is universal, and allows
  Scope to all such as feel the inherent glow—
Scott, Rogers, Campbell, Moore, and Crabbe, will try
'Gainst you the question with posterity.

8

For me who, wandering with pedestrian Muses,
  Contend not with you on the winged steed,

I wish your fate may yield ye, when she chooses,
    The fame you envy, and the skill you need;   60
And recollect a poet nothing loses
    In giving to his brethren their full meed
Of merit, and complaint of present days
Is not the *certain* path to future praise.

9

He that reserves his laurels for posterity
    (Who does not often claim the bright reversion?)
Has generally no great crop to spare it, he
    Being only injured by his own assertion;
And although here and there some glorious rarity
    Arise, like Titan from the sea's immersion,   70
The major part of such appellants go
To—God knows where—for no one else can know.

10

If, fallen in evil days, on evil tongues,
    Milton appeal'd to the Avenger, Time,
If Time, the Avenger, execrates his wrongs,
    And makes the word '*Miltonic*' mean '*sublime*',
He deign'd not to belie his soul in songs,
    Nor turn his very talent to a crime—
He did not loathe the sire to laud the son,
But closed the tyrant-hater he begun.   80

11

Think'st thou, could he, the blind Old Man, arise
    Like Samuel from the grave, to freeze once more
The blood of monarchs with his prophecies,
    Or be alive again—again all hoar
With time and trials, and those helpless eyes
    And heartless daughters, worn, and pale, and poor,
Would *he* adore a sultan? *he* obey
The intellectual eunuch Castlereagh?

12

Cold-blooded, smooth-faced, placid miscreant!
    Dabbling its sleek young hands in Erin's gore,   90

And thus for wider carnage taught to pant,
   Transferr'd to gorge upon a sister-shore;
The vulgarest tool that tyranny could want,
   With just enough of talent, and no more,
To lengthen fetters by another fix'd,
And offer poison long already mix'd.

13

An orator of such set trash of phrase
   Ineffably, legitimately vile,
That even its grossest flatterers dare not praise,
   Nor foes—all nations—condescend to smile: 100
Not even a *sprightly* blunder's spark can blaze
   From that Ixion grindstone's ceaseless toil,
That turns and turns, to give the world a notion
Of endless torments, and perpetual motion.

14

A bungler even in its disgusting trade,
   And botching, patching, leaving still behind
Something of which its masters are afraid,
   States to be curb'd, and thoughts to be confined,
Conspiracy or Congress to be made—
   Cobbling at manacles for all mankind—   110
A tinkering slavemaker, who mends old chains,
With God and man's abhorrence for its gains.

15

If we may judge of matter by the mind,
   Emasculated to the marrow, *It*
Hath but two objects—how to serve, and bind,
   Deeming the chain it wears even men may fit;
Eutropius of its many masters—blind
   To worth as freedom, wisdom as to wit—
Fearless, because *no* feeling dwells in ice,
Its very courage stagnates to a vice.   120

16

Where shall I turn me not to *view* its bonds?
   For I will never *feel* them—Italy!

Thy late reviving Roman soul desponds
   Beneath the lie this state-thing breathed o'er thee;
Thy clanking chain, and Erin's yet green wounds,
   Have voices—tongues to cry aloud for me.
Europe has slaves, allies, kings, armies still,
And Southey lives to sing them very ill.

17

Meantime, Sir Laureate, I proceed to dedicate
   In honest, simple verse, this song to you;   130
And if in flattering strains I do not predicate,
   'Tis that I still retain my 'buff and blue'.
My politics, as yet, are all to educate,
   Apostasy's so fashionable too,
To keep *one* creed's a task grown quite Herculean,
Is it not so, my Tory ultra-Julian?

.   .   .   .   .   .

from *Canto I*

[*Julia and Juan*]

75

Poor Julia's heart was in an awkward state;
   She felt it going, and resolved to make
The noblest efforts for herself and mate,
   For honour's, pride's, religion's, virtue's sake;
Her resolutions were most truly great,
   And almost might have made a Tarquin quake;
She pray'd the Virgin Mary for her grace,
As being the best judge of a lady's case.

76

She vow'd she never would see Juan more,
   And next day paid a visit to his mother,   10
And look'd extremely at the opening door,
   Which, by the Virgin's grace, let in another;

Grateful she was, and yet a little sore—
   Again it opens, it can be no other,
'Tis surely Juan now—No! I'm afraid
That night the Virgin was no further pray'd.

77

She now determined that a virtuous woman
   Should rather face and overcome temptation,
That flight was base and dastardly, and no man
   Should ever give her heart the least sensation;   20
That is to say, a thought beyond the common
   Preference, that we must feel upon occasion,
For people who are pleasanter than others,
But then they only seem so many brothers.

78

And even if by chance—and who can tell?
   The devil's so very sly—she should discover
That all within was not so very well,
   And, if still free, that such or such a lover
Might please perhaps, a virtuous wife can quell
   Such thoughts, and be the better when they're over;   30
And if the man should ask, 'tis but denial:
I recommend young ladies to make trial.

79

And then there are such things as love divine,
   Bright and immaculate, unmix'd and pure,
Such as the angels think so very fine,
   And matrons, who would be no less secure,
Platonic, perfect, 'just such love as mine':
   Thus Julia said—and thought so, to be sure,
And so I'd have her think, were I the man
On whom her reveries celestial ran.   40

80

Such love is innocent, and may exist
   Between young persons without any danger,
A hand may first, and then a lip be kist;

For my part, to such doings I'm a stranger,
But *hear* these freedoms form the utmost list
    Of all o'er which such love may be a ranger:
If people go beyond, 'tis quite a crime,
But not my fault—I tell them all in time.

81

Love, then, but love within its proper limits,
    Was Julia's innocent determination   50
In young Don Juan's favour, and to him its
    Exertion might be useful on occasion;
And, lighted at too pure a shrine to dim its
    Etherial lustre, with what sweet persuasion
He might be taught, by love and her together—
I really don't know what, nor Julia either.

82

Fraught with this fine intention, and well fenced
    In mail of proof—her purity of soul,
She, for the future of her strength convinced,
    And that her honour was a rock, or mole,   60
Exceeding sagely from that hour dispensed
    With any kind of troublesome control;
But whether Julia to the task was equal
Is that which must be mentioned in the sequel.

83

Her plan she deem'd both innocent and feasible,
    And, surely, with a stripling of sixteen
Not scandal's fangs could fix on much that's seizable,
    Or if they did so, satisfied to mean
Nothing but what was good, her breast was peaceable—
    A quiet conscience makes one so serene!   70
Christians have burnt each other, quite persuaded
That all the Apostles would have done as they did.

84

And if in the mean time her husband died,
    But heaven forbid that such a thought should cross

Her brain, though in a dream! (and then she sigh'd)
    Never could she survive that common loss;
But just suppose that moment should betide,
    I only say suppose it—*inter nos*—
(This should be *entre nous*, for Julia thought
In French, but then the rhyme would go for nought).   80

85

I only say suppose this supposition:
    Juan being then grown up to man's estate
Would fully suit a widow of condition,
    Even seven years hence it would not be too late;
And in the interim (to pursue this vision)
    The mischief, after all, could not be great,
For he would learn the rudiments of love,
I mean the seraph way of those above.

86

So much for Julia. Now we'll turn to Juan,
    Poor little fellow! he had no idea   90
Of his own case, and never hit the true one;
    In feelings quick as Ovid's Miss Medea,
He puzzled over what he found a new one,
    But not as yet imagined it could be a
Thing quite in course, and not at all alarming,
Which, with a little patience, might grow charming.

87

Silent and pensive, idle, restless, slow,
    His home deserted for the lonely wood,
Tormented with a wound he could not know,
    His, like all deep grief, plunged in solitude: 100
I'm fond myself of solitude or so,
    But then, I beg it may be understood,
By solitude I mean a sultan's, not
A hermit's, with a haram for a grot.

88

'Oh Love! in such a wilderness as this,
    Where transport and security entwine,

Here is the empire of thy perfect bliss,
  And here thou art a god indeed divine.'
The bard I quote from does not sing amiss,
  With the exception of the second line,   110
For that same twining 'transport and security'
Are twisted to a phrase of some obscurity.

89

The poet meant, no doubt, and thus appeals
  To the good sense and senses of mankind,
The very thing which every body feels,
  As all have found on trial, or may find,
That no one likes to be disturb'd at meals
  Or love.—I won't say more about 'entwined'
Or 'transport', as we knew all that before,
But beg 'Security' will bolt the door.   120

90

Young Juan wander'd by the glassy brooks
  Thinking unutterable things; he threw
Himself at length within the leafy nooks
  Where the wild branch of the cork forest grew;
There poets find materials for their books,
  And every now and then we read them through,
So that their plan and prosody are eligible,
Unless, like Wordsworth, they prove unintelligible.

91

He, Juan, (and not Wordsworth) so pursued
  His self-communion with his own high soul,   130
Until his mighty heart, in its great mood,
  Had mitigated part, though not the whole
Of its disease; he did the best he could
  With things not very subject to control,
And turn'd, without perceiving his condition,
Like Coleridge, into a metaphysician.

92

He thought about himself, and the whole earth,
  Of man the wonderful, and of the stars,

And how the deuce they ever could have birth;
　　And then he thought of earthquakes, and of wars,　　140
How many miles the moon might have in girth,
　　Of air-balloons, and of the many bars
To perfect knowledge of the boundless skies;
And then he thought of Donna Julia's eyes.

93

In thoughts like these true wisdom may discern
　　Longings sublime, and aspirations high,
Which some are born with, but the most part learn
　　To plague themselves withal, they know not why:
'Twas strange that one so young should thus concern
　　His brain about the action of the sky;　　　150
If *you* think 'twas philosophy that this did,
I can't help thinking puberty assisted.

94

He pored upon the leaves, and on the flowers,
　　And heard a voice in all the winds; and then
He thought of wood nymphs and immortal bowers,
　　And how the goddesses came down to men:
He miss'd the pathway, he forgot the hours,
　　And when he look'd upon his watch again,
He found how much old Time had been a winner—
He also found that he had lost his dinner.　　　160

95

Sometimes he turn'd to gaze upon his book,
　　Boscan, or Garcilasso;—by the wind
Even as the page is rustled while we look,
　　So by the poesy of his own mind
Over the mystic leaf his soul was shook,
　　As if 'twere one whereon magicians bind
Their spells, and give them to the passing gale,
According to some good old woman's tale.

96

Thus would he while his lonely hours away
　　Dissatisfied, nor knowing what he wanted;　　170

Nor glowing reverie, nor poet's lay,
 Could yield his spirit that for which it panted,
A bosom whereon he his head might lay,
 And hear the heart beat with the love it granted,
With——several other things, which I forget,
Or which, at least, I need not mention yet.

97

Those lonely walks, and lengthening reveries,
 Could not escape the gentle Julia's eyes;
She saw that Juan was not at his ease;
 But that which chiefly may, and must surprise, 180
Is, that the Donna Inez did not tease
 Her only son with question or surmise;
Whether it was she did not see, or would not,
Or, like all very clever people, could not.

98

This may seem strange, but yet 'tis very common;
 For instance—gentlemen, whose ladies take
Leave to o'erstep the written rights of woman,
 And break the———Which commandment is't they
  break?
(I have forgot the number, and think no man
 Should rashly quote, for fear of a mistake) 190
I say, when these same gentlemen are jealous,
They make some blunder, which their ladies tell us.

99

A real husband always is suspicious,
 But still no less suspects in the wrong place,
Jealous of some one who had no such wishes,
 Or pandering blindly to his own disgrace
By harbouring some dear friend extremely vicious;
 The last indeed's infallibly the case:
And when the spouse and friend are gone off wholly,
He wonders at their vice, and not his folly. 200

100

Thus parents also are at times short-sighted;
  Though watchful as the lynx, they ne'er discover,
The while the wicked world beholds delighted,
  Young Hopeful's mistress, or Miss Fanny's lover,
Till some confounded escapade has blighted
  The plan of twenty years, and all is over;
And then the mother cries, the father swears,
And wonders why the devil he got heirs.

101

But Inez was so anxious, and so clear
  Of sight, that I must think, on this occasion,
She had some other motive much more near
  For leaving Juan to this new temptation;
But what that motive was, I shan't say here;
  Perhaps to finish Juan's education,
Perhaps to open Don Alfonso's eyes,
In case he thought his wife too great a prize.

102

It was upon a day, a summer's day;—
  Summer's indeed a very dangerous season,
And so is spring about the end of May;
  The sun, no doubt, is the prevailing reason;
But whatsoe'er the cause is, one may say,
  And stand convicted of more truth than treason,
That there are months which nature grows more merry in,
March has its hares, and May must have its heroine.

103

'Twas on a summer's day—the sixth of June:—
  I like to be particular in dates,
Not only of the age, and year, but moon;
  They are a sort of post-house, where the Fates
Change horses, making history change its tune,
  Then spur away o'er empires and o'er states,
Leaving at last not much besides chronology,
Excepting the post-obits of theology.

104

'Twas on the sixth of June, about the hour
  Of half-past six—perhaps still nearer seven,
When Julia sate within as pretty a bower
  As e'er held houri in that heathenish heaven
Described by Mahomet, and Anacreon Moore,
  To whom the lyre and laurels have been given,
With all the trophies of triumphant song—
He won them well, and may he wear them long!   240

105

She sate, but not alone; I know not well
  How this same interview had taken place,
And even if I knew, I should not tell—
  People should hold their tongues in any case;
No matter how or why the thing befell,
  But there were she and Juan, face to face—
When two such faces are so, 'twould be wise,
But very difficult, to shut their eyes.

106

How beautiful she look'd! her conscious heart
  Glow'd in her cheek, and yet she felt no wrong.   250
Oh Love! how perfect is thy mystic art,
  Strengthening the weak, and trampling on the strong,
How self-deceitful is the sagest part
  Of mortals whom thy lure hath led along—
The precipice she stood on was immense,
So was her creed in her own innocence.

107

She thought of her own strength, and Juan's youth,
  And of the folly of all prudish fears,
Victorious virtue, and domestic truth,
  And then of Don Alfonso's fifty years;   260
I wish these last had not occurr'd, in sooth,
  Because that number rarely much endears,
And through all climes, the snowy and the sunny,
Sounds ill in love, whate'er it may in money.

108

When people say, 'I've told you *fifty* times,'
  They mean to scold, and very often do;
When poets say, 'I've written *fifty* rhymes,'
  They make you dread that they'll recite them too;
In gangs of *fifty*, thieves commit their crimes;
  At *fifty* love for love is rare, 'tis true,   270
But then, no doubt, it equally as true is,
A good deal may be bought for *fifty* Louis.

109

Julia had honour, virtue, truth, and love,
  For Don Alfonso; and she inly swore,
By all the vows below to powers above,
  She never would disgrace the ring she wore,
Nor leave a wish which wisdom might reprove;
  And while she ponder'd this, besides much more,
One hand on Juan's carelessly was thrown,
Quite by mistake—she thought it was her own;   280

110

Unconsciously she lean'd upon the other,
  Which play'd within the tangles of her hair;
And to contend with thoughts she could not smother,
  She seem'd by the distraction of her air.
'Twas surely very wrong in Juan's mother
  To leave together this imprudent pair,
She who for many years had watch'd her son so—
I'm very certain *mine* would not have done so.

111

The hand which still held Juan's, by degrees
  Gently, but palpably confirm'd its grasp,   290
As if it said 'detain me, if you please';
  Yet there's no doubt she only meant to clasp
His fingers with a pure Platonic squeeze;
  She would have shrunk as from a toad, or asp,
Had she imagined such a thing could rouse
A feeling dangerous to a prudent spouse.

112

I cannot know what Juan thought of this,
   But what he did, is much what you would do;
His young lip thank'd it with a grateful kiss,
   And then, abash'd at its own joy, withdrew   300
In deep despair, lest he had done amiss,
   Love is so very timid when 'tis new:
She blush'd, and frown'd not, but she strove to speak,
And held her tongue, her voice was grown so weak.

113

The sun set, and up rose the yellow moon:
   The devil's in the moon for mischief; they
Who call'd her CHASTE, methinks, began too soon
   Their nomenclature; there is not a day,
The longest, not the twenty-first of June,
   Sees half the business in a wicked way   310
On which three single hours of moonshine smile—
And then she looks so modest all the while.

114

There is a dangerous silence in that hour,
   A stillness, which leaves room for the full soul
To open all itself, without the power
   Of calling wholly back its self-control;
The silver light which, hallowing tree and tower,
   Sheds beauty and deep softness o'er the whole,
Breathes also to the heart, and o'er it throws
A loving languor, which is not repose.   320

115

And Julia sate with Juan, half embraced
   And half retiring from the glowing arm,
Which trembled like the bosom where 'twas placed;
   Yet still she must have thought there was no harm,
Or else 'twere easy to withdraw her waist;
   But then the situation had its charm,
And then——God knows what next—I can't go on;
I'm almost sorry that I e'er begun.

116

Oh Plato! Plato! you have paved the way,
   With your confounded fantasies, to more   330
Immoral conduct by the fancied sway
   Your system feigns o'er the controlless core
Of human hearts, than all the long array
   Of poets and romancers:—You're a bore,
A charlatan, a coxcomb—and have been,
At best, no better than a go-between.

117

And Julia's voice was lost, except in sighs,
   Until too late for useful conversation;
The tears were gushing from her gentle eyes,
   I wish, indeed, they had not had occasion,   340
But who, alas! can love, and then be wise?
   Not that remorse did not oppose temptation,
A little still she strove, and much repented,
And whispering 'I will ne'er consent'—consented.

118

'Tis said that Xerxes offer'd a reward
   To those who could invent him a new pleasure;
Methinks, the requisition's rather hard,
   And must have cost his majesty a treasure:
For my part, I'm a moderate-minded bard,
   Fond of a little love (which I call leisure);   350
I care not for new pleasures, as the old
Are quite enough for me, so they but hold.

119

Oh Pleasure! you're indeed a pleasant thing,
   Although one must be damn'd for you, no doubt;
I make a resolution every spring
   Of reformation, ere the year run out,
But, somehow, this my vestal vow takes wing,
   Yet still, I trust, it may be kept throughout:
I'm very sorry, very much ashamed,
And mean, next winter, to be quite reclaim'd.   360

[Julia's Farewell Letter]

192

'They tell me 'tis decided; you depart:
  'Tis wise—'tis well, but not the less a pain;
I have no further claim on your young heart,
  Mine was the victim, and would be again;
To love too much has been the only art
  I used;—I write in haste, and if a stain
Be on this sheet, 'tis not what it appears,
My eyeballs burn and throb, but have no tears.

193

'I loved, I love you, for that love have lost
  State, station, heaven, mankind's, my own esteem,   370
And yet can not regret what it hath cost,
  So dear is still the memory of that dream;
Yet, if I name my guilt, 'tis not to boast,
  None can deem harshlier of me than I deem:
I trace this scrawl because I cannot rest—
I've nothing to reproach, nor to request.

194

'Man's love is of his life a thing apart,
  'Tis woman's whole existence; man may range
The court, camp, church, the vessel, and the mart,
  Sword, gown, gain, glory, offer in exchange   380
Pride, fame, ambition, to fill up his heart,
  And few there are whom these can not estrange;
Man has all these resources, we but one,
To love again, and be again undone.

195

'My breast has been all weakness, is so yet;
  I struggle, but cannot collect my mind;
My blood still rushes where my spirit's set,
  As roll the waves before the settled wind;
My brain is feminine, nor can forget—
  To all, except your image, madly blind;   390

As turns the needle trembling to the pole
It ne'er can reach, so turns to you, my soul.

196

'You will proceed in beauty, and in pride,
    Beloved and loving many; all is o'er
For me on earth, except some years to hide
    My shame and sorrow deep in my heart's core;
These I could bear, but cannot cast aside
    The passion which still rends it as before,
And so farewell—forgive me, love me—No,
That word is idle now—but let it go.   400

197

'I have no more to say, but linger still,
    And dare not set my seal upon this sheet,
And yet I may as well the task fulfil,
    My misery can scarce be more complete:
I had not lived till now, could sorrow kill;
    Death flies the wretch who fain the blow would meet,
And I must even survive this last adieu,
And bear with life, to love and pray for you!'

198

This note was written upon gilt-edged paper
    With a neat crow-quill, rather hard, but new;   410
Her small white fingers scarce could reach the taper,
    But trembled as magnetic needles do,
And yet she did not let one tear escape her;
    The seal a sunflower; '*Elle vous suit partout*',
The motto, cut upon a white cornelian;
The wax was superfine, its hue vermilion.

                                        [1819]

from *Canto III*

[Haidée's and Juan's Feast]

67

Haidée and Juan carpeted their feet
  On crimson satin, border'd with pale blue;
Their sofa occupied three parts complete
  Of the apartment—and appear'd quite new;
The velvet cushions—(for a throne more meet)—
  Were scarlet, from whose glowing centre grew
A sun emboss'd in gold, whose rays of tissue,
Meridian-like, were seen all light to issue.

68

Crystal and marble, plate and porcelain,
  Had done their work of splendour; Indian mats   10
And Persian carpets, which the heart bled to stain,
  Over the floors were spread; gazelles and cats,
And dwarfs and blacks, and such like things, that gain
  Their bread as ministers and favourites—(that's
To say, by degradation)—mingled there
As plentiful as in a court or fair.

69

There was no want of lofty mirrors, and
  The tables, most of ebony inlaid
With mother of pearl or ivory, stood at hand,
  Or were of tortoise-shell or rare woods made,   20
Fretted with gold or silver:—by command
  The greater part of these were ready spread
With viands and sherbets in ice—and wine—
Kept for all comers, at all hours to dine.

70

Of all the dresses I select Haidée's:
  She wore two jelicks—one was of pale yellow;
Of azure, pink, and white was her chemise—

'Neath which her breast heaved like a little billow;
With buttons form'd of pearls as large as peas,
  All gold and crimson shone her jelick's fellow,   30
And the striped white gauze baracan that bound her
Like fleecy clouds about the moon, flow'd round her.

71

One large gold bracelet clasp'd each lovely arm,
  Lockless—so pliable from the pure gold
That the hand stretch'd and shut it without harm,
  The limb which it adorn'd its only mould;
So beautiful—its very shape would charm,
  And clinging as if loth to lose its hold,
The purest ore enclosed the whitest skin
That e'er by precious metal was held in.   40

72

Around, as princess of her father's land,
  A like gold bar above her instep roll'd
Announced her rank; twelve rings were on her hand;
  Her hair was starr'd with gems; her veil's fine fold
Below her breast was fasten'd with a band
  Of lavish pearls, whose worth could scarce be told;
Her orange silk full Turkish trousers furl'd
About the prettiest ankle in the world.

73

Her hair's auburn waves down to her heel
  Flow'd like an Alpine torrent which the sun   50
Dyes with his morning light,—and would conceal
  Her person if allow'd at large to run,
And still they seem resentfully to feel
  The silken fillet's curb, and sought to shun
Their bonds whene'er some Zephyr caught began
To offer his young pinion as her fan.

74

Round her she made an atmosphere of life,
  The very air seem'd lighter from her eyes,

They were so soft and beautiful, and rife
  With all we can imagine of the skies,   60
And pure as Psyche ere she grew a wife—
  Too pure even for the purest human ties;
Her overpowering presence made you feel
It would not be idolatry to kneel.

75

Her eyelashes, though dark as night, were tinged
  (It is the country's custom), but in vain;
For those large black eyes were so blackly fringed,
  The glossy rebels mock'd the jetty stain,
And in their native beauty stood avenged:
  Her nails were touch'd with henna; but again   70
The power of art was turn'd to nothing, for
They could not look more rosy than before.

76

The henna should be deeply dyed to make
  The skin relieved appear more fairly fair;
She had no need of this, day ne'er will break
  On mountain tops more heavenly white than her:
The eye might doubt if it were well awake,
  She was so like a vision; I might err,
But Shakespeare also says 'tis very silly,
'To gild refined gold, or paint the lily'.   80

77

Juan had on a shawl of black and gold,
  But a white baracan, and so transparent
The sparkling gems beneath you might behold,
  Like small stars through the milky way apparent;
His turban, furl'd in many a graceful fold,
  An emerald aigrette with Haidée's hair in't
Surmounted as its clasp—a glowing crescent,
Whose rays shone ever trembling, but incessant.

78

And now they were diverted by their suite,
  Dwarfs, dancing girls, black eunuchs, and a poet,   90

Which made their new establishment complete;
    The last was of great fame, and liked to show it:
His verses rarely wanted their due feet—
    And for his theme—he seldom sung below it,
He being paid to satirize or flatter,
As the psalm says, 'inditing a good matter.'

79

He praised the present, and abused the past,
    Reversing the good custom of old days,
An eastern antijacobin at last
    He turn'd, preferring pudding to *no* praise—   100
For some few years his lot had been o'ercast
    By his seeming independent in his lays,
But now he sung the Sultan and the Pacha
With truth like Southey and with verse like Crashaw.

80

He was a man who had seen many changes,
    And always changed as true as any needle;
His polar star being one which rather ranges,
    And not the fix'd—he knew the way to wheedle:
So vile, he 'scaped the doom which oft avenges;
    And being fluent (save indeed when fee'd ill),   110
He lied with such a fervour of intention—
There was no doubt he earn'd his laureate pension.

81

But he had genius,—when a turncoat has it
    The 'Vates irritabilis' takes care
That without notice few full moons shall pass it;
    Even good men like to make the public stare:—
But to my subject—let me see—what was it?—
    Oh!—the third canto—and the pretty pair—
Their loves, and feasts, and house, and dress, and mode
Of living in their insular abode.   120

82

Their poet, a sad trimmer, but no less
    In company a very pleasant fellow,

Had been the favourite of full many a mess
   Of men, and made them speeches when half mellow;
And though his meaning they could rarely guess,
   Yet still they deign'd to hiccup or to bellow
The glorious meed of popular applause,
Of which the first ne'er knows the second cause.

83

But now being lifted into high society,
   And having pick'd up several odds and ends   130
Of free thoughts in his travels, for variety,
   He deem'd, being in a lone isle, among friends,
That without any danger of a riot, he
   Might for long lying make himself amends;
And singing as he sung in his warm youth,
Agree to a short armistice with truth.

84

He had travell'd 'mongst the Arabs, Turks, and Franks,
   And knew the self-loves of the different nations;
And having lived with people of all ranks,
   Had something ready upon most occasions—   140
Which got him a few presents and some thanks.
   He varied with some skill his adulations;
To 'do at Rome as Romans do', a piece
Of conduct was which he observed in Greece.

85

Thus, usually, when he was ask'd to sing,
   He gave the different nations something national;
'Twas all the same to him—'God save the king,'
   Or 'Ça ira', according to the fashion all;
His muse made increment of any thing,
   From the high lyric down to the low rational: 150
If Pindar sang horse-races, what should hinder
Himself from being as pliable as Pindar?

86

In France, for instance, he would write a chanson;
   In England, a six canto quarto tale;

In Spain, he'd made a ballad or romance on
   The last war—much the same in Portugal;
In Germany, the Pegasus he'd prance on
   Would be old Goethe's—(see what says de Staël)
In Italy, he'd ape the 'Trecentisti';
In Greece, he'd sing some sort of hymn like this t'ye: 160

1

   The isles of Greece, the isles of Greece!
      Where burning Sappho loved and sung,
   Where grew the arts of war and peace,—
      Where Delos rose, and Phoebus sprung!
   Eternal summer gilds them yet,
   But all, except their sun, is set.

2

   The Scian and the Teian muse,
      The hero's harp, the lover's lute,
   Have found the fame your shores refuse;
      Their place of birth alone is mute   170
   To sounds which echo further west
   Than your sires' 'Islands of the Blest'.

3

   The mountains look on Marathon—
      And Marathon looks on the sea;
   And musing there an hour alone,
      I dream'd that Greece might still be free;
   For standing on the Persian's grave,
   I could not deem myself a slave.

4

   A king sate on the rocky brow
      Which looks o'er sea-born Salamis;   180
   And ships, by thousands, lay below,
      And men in nations;—all were his!
   He counted them at break of day—
   And when the sun set where were they?

5

And where are they? and where art thou,
  My country? On thy voiceless shore
The heroic lay is tuneless now—
  The heroic bosom beats no more!
And must thy lyre, so long divine,
Degenerate into hands like mine?   190

6

'Tis something, in the dearth of fame,
  Though link'd among a fetter'd race,
To feel at least a patriot's shame,
  Even as I sing, suffuse my face;
For what is left the poet here?
For Greeks a blush—for Greece a tear.

7

Must *we* but weep o'er days more blest?
  Must *we* but blush?—Our fathers bled.
Earth! render back from out thy breast
  A remnant of our Spartan dead!   200
Of the three hundred grant but three,
To make a new Thermopylae!

8

What, silent still? and silent all?
  Ah! no;—the voices of the dead
Sounds like a distant torrent's fall,
  And answer, 'Let one living head,
But one arise,—we come, we come!'
'Tis but the living who are dumb.

9

In vain—in vain: strike other chords:
  Fill high the cup with Samian wine!   210
Leave battles to the Turkish hordes,
  And shed the blood of Scio's vine!
Hark! rising to the ignoble call—
How answers each bold bacchanal!

10

You have the Pyrrhic dance as yet,
    Where is the Pyrrhic phalanx gone?
Of two such lessons, why forget
    The nobler and the manlier one?
You have the letters Cadmus gave—
Think ye he meant them for a slave?   220

11

Fill high the bowl with Samian wine!
    We will not think of themes like these!
It made Anacreon's song divine:
    He served—but served Polycrates—
A tyrant; but our masters then
Were still, at least, our countrymen.

12

The tyrant of the Chersonese
    Was freedom's best and bravest friend;
That tyrant was Miltiades!
    Oh! that the present hour would lend   230
Another despot of the kind!
Such chains as his were sure to bind.

13

Fill high the bowl with Samian wine!
    On Suli's rock, and Parga's shore,
Exists the remnant of a line
    Such as the Doric mothers bore;
And there, perhaps, some seed is sown,
The Heracleidan blood might own.

14

Trust not for freedom to the Franks—
    They have a king who buys and sells: 240
In native swords, and native ranks,
    The only hope of courage dwells;
But Turkish force, and Latin fraud,
Would break your shield, however broad.

15

Fill high the bowl with Samian wine!
 Our virgins dance beneath the shade—
I see their glorious black eyes shine;
 But gazing on each glowing maid,
My own the burning tear-drop laves,
To think such breasts must suckle slaves.   250

16

Place me on Sunium's marbled steep,
 Where nothing, save the waves and I,
May hear our mutual murmurs sweep;
 There, swan-like, let me sing and die:
A land of slaves shall ne'er be mine—
Dash down yon cup of Samian wine!

87

Thus sung, or would, or could, or should have sung,
 The modern Greek, in tolerable verse;
If not like Orpheus quite, when Greece was young,
 Yet in these times he might have done much worse: 260
His strain display'd some feeling—right or wrong;
 And feeling, in a poet, is the source
Of others' feeling; but they are such liars,
And take all colours—like the hands of dyers.

88

But words are things, and a small drop of ink,
 Falling like dew, upon a thought, produces
That which makes thousands, perhaps millions, think;
 'Tis strange, the shortest letter which man uses
Instead of speech, may form a lasting link
 Of ages; to what straits old Time reduces 270
Frail man, when paper—even a rag like this,
Survives himself, his tomb, and all that's his.

89

And when his bones are dust, his grave a blank,
 His station, generation, even his nation,

Become a thing, or nothing, save to rank
    In chronological commemoration
Some dull MS oblivion long has sank,
    Or graven stone found in a barrack's station
In digging the foundation of a closet,
May turn his name up, as a rare deposit.   280

90

And glory long has made the sages smile;
    'Tis something, nothing, words, illusion, wind—
Depending more upon the historian's style
    Than on the name a person leaves behind:
Troy owes to Homer what whist owes to Hoyle;
    The present century was growing blind
To the great Marlborough's skill in giving knocks,
Until his late Life by Archdeacon Coxe.

91

Milton's the prince of poets—so we say;
    A little heavy, but no less divine: 290
An independent being in his day—
    Learn'd, pious, temperate in love and wine;
But his life falling into Johnson's way,
    We're told this great high priest of all the Nine
Was whipt at college—a harsh sire—odd spouse,
For the first Mrs Milton left his house.

92

All these are, *certes*, entertaining facts,
    Like Shakespeare's stealing deer, Lord Bacon's bribes;
Like Titus' youth, and Caesar's earliest acts;
    Like Burns (whom Doctor Currie well describes);   300
Like Cromwell's pranks;—but although truth exacts
    These amiable descriptions from the scribes,
As most essential to their hero's story,
They do not much contribute to his glory.

93

All are not moralists, like Southey, when
    He prated to the world of 'Pantisocrasy';

Or Wordsworth unexcised, unhired, who then
   Season'd his pedlar poems with democracy;
Or Coleridge, long before his flighty pen
   Lent to the Morning Post its aristocracy;   310
When he and Southey, following the same path,
Espoused two partners (milliners of Bath.)

94

Such names at present cut a convict figure,
   The very Botany Bay in moral geography;
Their loyal treason, renegado rigour,
   Are good manure for their more bare biography.
Wordsworth's last quarto, by the way, is bigger
   Than any since the birthday of typography;
A drowsy frowzy poem, call'd the 'Excursion',
Writ in a manner which is my aversion.   320

95

He there builds up a formidable dyke
   Between his own and others' intellect;
But Wordsworth's poem, and his followers, like
   Joanna Southcote's Shiloh, and her sect,
Are things which in this century don't strike
   The public mind, so few are the elect;
And the new births of both their stale virginities
Have proved but dropsies, taken for divinities.

96

But let me to my story: I must own,
   If I have any fault, it is digression;   330
Leaving my people to proceed alone,
   While I soliloquize beyond expression;
But these are my addresses from the throne,
   Which put off business to the ensuing session:
Forgetting each omission is a loss to
The World, not quite so great as Ariosto.

[1821]

from *Canto IV*

[*The Death of Haidée*]

54

I leave Don Juan for the present, safe—
   Not sound, poor fellow, but severely wounded;
Yet could his corporal pangs amount to half
   Of those with which his Haidée's bosom bounded!
She was not one to weep, and rave, and chafe,
   And then give way, subdued because surrounded;
Her mother was a Moorish maid, from Fez,
Where all is Eden, or a wilderness.

55

There the large olive rains its amber store
   In marble fonts; there grain, and flower, and fruit,   10
Gush from the earth until the land runs o'er;
   But there too many a poison-tree has root,
And midnight listens to the lion's roar,
   And long, long deserts scorch the camel's foot,
Or heaving whelm the helpless caravan,
And as the soil is, so the heart of man.

56

Afric is all the sun's, and as her earth
   Her human clay is kindled; full of power
For good or evil, burning from its birth,
   The Moorish blood partakes the planet's hour,   20
And like the soil beneath it will bring forth:
   Beauty and love were Haidée's mother's dower;
But her large dark eye show'd deep Passion's force,
Though sleeping like a lion near a source.

57

Her daughter, temper'd with a milder ray,
   Like summer clouds all silvery, smooth, and fair,
Till slowly charged with thunder they display

Terror to earth, and tempest to the air,
Had held till now her soft and milky way;
  But overwrought with passion and despair,   30
The fire burst forth from her Numidian veins,
Even as the Simoom sweeps the blasted plains.

58

The last sight which she saw was Juan's gore,
  And he himself o'ermaster'd and cut down;
His blood was running on the very floor
  Where late he trod, her beautiful, her own;
Thus much she view'd an instant and no more,—
  Her struggles ceased with one convulsive groan;
On her sire's arm, which until now scarce held
Her writhing, fell she like a cedar fell'd.   40

59

A vein had burst, and her sweet lips' pure dyes
  Were dabbled with the deep blood which ran o'er;
And her head droop'd as when the lily lies
  O'ercharged with rain: her summon'd handmaids bore
Their lady to her couch with gushing eyes;
  Of herbs and cordials they produced their store,
But she defied all means they could employ,
Like one life could not hold, nor death destroy.

60

Days lay she in that state unchanged, though chill
  With nothing livid, still her lips were red;   50
She had no pulse, but death seem'd absent still;
  No hideous sign proclaim'd her surely dead;
Corruption came not in each mind to kill
  All hope; to look upon her sweet face bred
New thoughts of life, for it seem'd full of soul,
She had so much, earth could not claim the whole.

61

The ruling passion, such as marble shows
  When exquisitely chisell'd, still lay there,

But fix'd as marble's unchanged aspect throws
   O'er the fair Venus, but for ever fair;   60
O'er the Laocoon's all eternal throes,
   And ever-dying Gladiator's air,
Their energy like life forms all their fame,
Yet looks not life, for they are still the same.

62

She woke at length, but not as sleepers wake,
   Rather the dead, for life seem'd something new,
A strange sensation which she must partake
   Perforce, since whatsoever met her view
Struck not on memory, though a heavy ache
   Lay at her heart, whose earliest beat still true   70
Brought back the sense of pain without the cause,
For, for a while, the furies made a pause.

63

She look'd on many a face with vacant eye,
   On many a token without knowing what;
She saw them watch her without asking why,
   And reck'd not who around her pillow sat;
Not speechless though she spoke not; not a sigh
   Relieved her thoughts; dull silence and quick chat
Were tried in vain by those who served; she gave
No sign, save breath, of having left the grave.   80

64

Her handmaids tended, but she heeded not;
   Her father watch'd, she turn'd her eyes away;
She recognized no being, and no spot
   However dear or cherish'd in their day;
They changed from room to room, but all forgot,
   Gentle, but without memory she lay;
At length those eyes, which they would fain be weaning
Back to old thoughts, wax'd full of fearful meaning.

65

And then a slave bethought her of a harp;
   The harper came, and tuned his instrument;   90

At the first notes, irregular and sharp,
  On him her flashing eyes a moment bent,
Then to the wall she turn'd as if to warp
  Her thoughts from sorrow through her heart re-sent,
And he begun a long low island song
Of ancient days, ere tyranny grew strong.

66

Anon her thin wan fingers beat the wall
  In time to his old tune; he changed the theme,
And sung of love; the fierce name struck through all
  Her recollection; on her flash'd the dream   100
Of what she was, and is, if ye could call
  To be so being; in a gushing stream
The tears rush'd forth from her o'erclouded brain,
Like mountain mists at length dissolved in rain.

67

Short solace, vain relief!—thought came too quick,
  And whirl'd her brain to madness; she arose
As one who ne'er had dwelt among the sick,
  And flew at all she met, as on her foes;
But no one ever heard her speak or shriek,
  Although her paroxysm drew towards its close: 110
Hers was a phrensy which disdain'd to rave,
Even when they smote her, in the hope to save.

68

Yet she betray'd at times a gleam of sense;
  Nothing could make her meet her father's face,
Though on all other things with looks intense
  She gazed, but none she ever could retrace;
Food she refused, and raiment; no pretence
  Avail'd for either; neither change of place,
Nor time, nor skill, nor remedy, could give her
Senses to sleep—the power seem'd gone for ever.   120

69

Twelve days and nights she wither'd thus; at last,
  Without a groan, or sigh, or glance, to show

A parting pang, the spirit from her past:
    And they who watch'd her nearest could not know
The very instant, till the change that cast
    Her sweet face into shadow, dull and slow,
Glazed o'er her eyes—the beautiful, the black—
Oh! to possess such lustre—and then lack!

70

She died, but not alone; she held within
    A second principle of life, which might   130
Have dawn'd a fair and sinless child of sin;
    But closed its little being without light,
And went down to the grave unborn, wherein
    Blossom and bough lie wither'd with one blight;
In vain the dews of Heaven descend above
The bleeding flower and blasted fruit of love.

[1821]

Canto XI

1

When Bishop Berkeley said 'there was no matter',
    And proved it—'twas no matter what he said:
They say his system 'tis in vain to batter,
    Too subtle for the airiest human head;
And yet who can believe it! I would shatter
    Gladly all matters, down to stone or lead,
Or adamant, to find the World a spirit,
And wear my head, denying that I wear it.

2

What a sublime discovery 'twas to make the
    Universe universal Egotism!   10
That all's ideal—*all ourselves*: I'll stake the
    World (be it what you will) that *that's* no Schism.
Oh, Doubt!—if thou be'st Doubt, for which some take thee,
    But which I doubt extremely—thou sole prism

Of the Truth's rays, spoil not my draught of spirit!
Heaven's brandy,—though our brain can hardly bear it.

3

For ever and anon comes Indigestion,
   (Not the most 'dainty Ariel') and perplexes
Our soarings with another sort of question:
   And that which after all my spirit vexes,   20
Is, that I find no spot where man can rest eye on,
   Without confusion of the sorts and sexes,
Of being, stars, and this unriddled wonder,
The World, which at the worst's a glorious blunder—

4

If it be Chance; or if it be according
   To the Old Text, still better:—lest it should
Turn out so, we'll say nothing 'gainst the wording,
   As several people think such hazards rude:
They're right; our days are too brief for affording
   Space to dispute what *no one* ever could   30
Decide, and *every body one day* will
Know very clearly—or at least lie still.

5

And therefore will I leave off metaphysical
   Discussion, which is neither here nor there:
If I agree that what is, is; then this I call
   Being quite perspicuous and extremely fair.
The truth is, I've grown lately rather phthisical:
   I don't know what the reason is—the air
Perhaps; but as I suffer from the shocks
Of illness, I grow much more orthodox.   40

6

The first attack at once proved the Divinity
   (But *that* I never doubted, nor the Devil);
The next, the Virgin's mystical virginity;
   The third, the usual Origin of Evil;
The fourth at once established the whole Trinity

On so uncontrovertible a level,
That I devoutly wished the three were four,
On purpose to believe so much the more.

7

To our theme:—The man who has stood on the Acropolis,
    And looked down over Attica; or he   50
Who has sailed where picturesque Constantinople is,
    Or seen Timbuctoo, or hath taken tea
In small-eyed China's crockery-ware metropolis,
    Or sat amidst the bricks of Nineveh,
May not think much of London's first appearance—
But ask him what he thinks of it a year hence?

8

Don Juan had got out on Shooter's Hill;
    Sunset the time, the place the same declivity
Which looks along that vale of good and ill
    Where London streets ferment in full activity;   60
While every thing around was calm and still,
    Except the creak of wheels, which on their pivot he
Heard,—and that bee-like, bubbling, busy hum
Of cities, that boil over with their scum:—

9

I say, Don Juan, wrapt in contemplation,
    Walked on behind his carriage, o'er the summit,
And lost in wonder of so great a nation,
    Gave way to't, since he could not overcome it.
'And here,' he cried, 'is Freedom's chosen station;
    Here peals the people's voice, nor can entomb it   70
Racks, prisons, inquisitions; resurrection
Awaits it, each new meeting or election.

10

'Here are chaste wives, pure lives; here people pay
    But what they please; and if that things be dear,
'Tis only that they love to throw away
    Their cash, to show how much they have a-year.

Here laws are all inviolate; none lay
   Traps for the traveller; every highway's clear:
Here'——he was interrupted by a knife,
With, 'Damn your eyes! your money or your life!'   80

11

These freeborn sounds proceeded from four pads,
   In ambush laid, who had perceived him loiter
Behind his carriage; and, like handy lads,
   Had seized the lucky hour to reconnoitre,
In which the heedless gentleman who gads
   Upon the road, unless he prove a fighter,
May find himself within that Isle of riches
Exposed to lose his life as well as breeches.

12

Juan, who did not understand a word
   Of English, save their shibboleth, 'God damn!'   90
And even that he had so rarely heard,
   He sometimes thought 'twas only their 'Salām,'
Or 'God be with you!'—and 'tis not absurd
   To think so; for half English as I am
(To my misfortune) never can I say
I heard them wish 'God with you,' save that way;—

13

Juan yet quickly understood their gesture,
   And being somewhat choleric and sudden,
Drew forth a pocket-pistol from his vesture,
   And fired it into one assailant's pudding—   100
Who fell, as rolls an ox o'er in his pasture,
   And roared out, as he writhed his native mud in,
Unto his nearest follower or henchman,
'Oh Jack! I'm floored by that 'ere bloody Frenchman!'

14

On which Jack and his train set off at speed,
   And Juan's suite, late scattered at a distance,
Came up, all marvelling at such a deed,

And offering, as usual, late assistance.
Juan, who saw the Moon's late minion bleed
    As if his veins would pour out his existence,   110
Stood calling out for bandages and lint,
And wished he had been less hasty with his flint.

15

'Perhaps,' thought he, 'it is the country's Wont
    To welcome foreigners in this way: now
I recollect some innkeepers who don't
    Differ, except in robbing with a bow,
In lieu of a bare blade and brazen front.
    But what is to be done? I can't allow
The fellow to lie groaning on the road:
So take him up; I'll help you with the load.'   120

16

But ere they could perform this pious duty,
    The dying man cried, 'Hold! I've got my gruel!
Oh! for a glass of *max*! We've miss'd our booty—
    Let me die where I am!' And as the fuel
Of life shrunk in his heart, and thick and sooty
    The drops fell from his death-wound, and he drew ill
His breath,—he from his swelling throat untied
A kerchief, crying 'Give Sal that!'—and died.

17

The cravat stained with bloody drops fell down
    Before Don Juan's feet: he could not tell   130
Exactly why it was before him thrown,
    Nor what the meaning of the man's farewell.
Poor Tom was once a kiddy upon town,
    A thorough varmint, and a *real* swell,
Full flash, all fancy, until fairly diddled,
His pockets first, and then his body riddled.

18

Don Juan, having done the best he could
    In all the circumstances of the case,

As soon as 'Crowner's 'quest' allowed, pursued
  His travels to the capital apace;—   140
Esteeming it a little hard he should
  In twelve hours' time, and very little space,
Have been obliged to slay a freeborn native
In self-defence:—this made him meditative.

19

He from the world had cut off a great man,
  Who in his time had made heroic bustle.
Who in a row like Tom could lead the van,
  Booze in the ken, or at the spellken hustle?
Who queer a flat? Who (spite of Bow-street's ban)
  On the high toby-spice so flash the muzzle?   150
Who on a lark, with black-eyed Sal (his blowing)
So prime, so swell, so nutty, and so knowing?

20

But Tom's no more—and so no more of Tom.
  Heroes must die; and by God's blessing 'tis
Not long before the most of them go home.—
  Hail! Thamis, hail! Upon thy verge it is
That Juan's chariot, rolling like a drum
  In thunder, holds the way it can't well miss,
Through Kennington and all the other 'tons,'
Which make us wish ourselves in town at once;—   160

21

Through Groves, so called as being void of trees,
  (Like *lucus* from *no* light); through prospects named
Mounts Pleasant, as containing nought to please,
  Nor much to climb; through little boxes framed
Of bricks, to let the dust in at your ease,
  With 'To be let,' upon their doors proclaimed;
Through 'Rows' most modestly called 'Paradise,'
Which Eve might quit without much sacrifice;—

22

Through coaches, drays, choked turnpikes, and a whirl
  Of wheels, and roar of voices and confusion;   170

Here taverns wooing to a pint of 'purl',
   There mails fast flying off like a delusion;
There barber's blocks with periwigs in curl
   In windows; here the lamplighter's infusion
Slowly distilled into the glimmering glass,
(For in those days we had not got to gas:)—

23

Through this, and much, and more, is the approach
   Of travellers to mighty Babylon:
Whether they come by horse, or chaise, or coach,
   With slight exceptions, all the ways seem one.   180
I could say more, but do not choose to encroach
   Upon the guide-book's privilege. The Sun
Had set some time, and night was on the ridge
Of twilight, as the party crossed the bridge.

24

That's rather fine, the gentle sound of Thamis—
   Who vindicates a moment too his stream—
Though hardly heard through multifarious 'damme's.'
   The lamps of Westminster's more regular gleam,
The breadth of pavement, and yon shrine where Fame is
   A spectral resident—whose pallid beam   190
In shape of moonshine hovers o'er the pile—
Make this a sacred part of Albion's Isle.

25

The Druid's groves are gone—so much the better:
   Stone-Henge is not—but what the devil is it?—
But Bedlam still exists with its sage fetter,
   That madmen may not bite you on a visit;
The Bench too seats or suits full many a debtor;
   The Mansion House too (though some people quiz it)
To me appears a stiff yet grand erection;
But then the Abbey's worth the whole collection.   200

26

The line of lights too up to Charing Cross,
   Pall Mall, and so forth, have a coruscation

Like gold as in comparison to dross,
   Matched with the Continent's illumination,
Whose cities Night by no means deigns to gloss:
   The French were not yet a lamp-lighting nation,
And when they grew so—on their new-found lanthorn,
Instead of wicks, they made a wicked man turn.

27

A row of gentlemen along the streets
   Suspended, may illuminate mankind,   210
As also bonfires made of country seats;
   But the old way is best for the purblind:
The other looks like phosphorus on sheets,
   A sort of Ignis-fatuus to the mind,
Which, though 'tis certain to perplex and frighten,
Must burn more mildly ere it can enlighten.

28

But London's so well lit, that if Diogenes
   Could recommence to hunt his *honest man*,
And found him not amidst the various progenies
   Of this enormous city's spreading spawn,   220
'Twere not for want of lamps to aid his dodging his
   Yet undiscovered treasure. What *I* can,
I've done to find the same throughout life's journey,
But see the world is only one attorney.

29

Over the stones still rattling up Pall Mall,
   Through crowds and carriages, but waxing thinner
As thundered knockers broke the long-sealed spell
   Of doors 'gainst duns, and to an early dinner
Admitted a small party as night fell,—
   Don Juan, our young diplomatic sinner,   230
Pursued his path, and drove past some Hotels,
St James's Palace, and St James's 'Hells'.

30

They reached the hotel: forth streamed from the front door
   A tide of well-clad waiters, and around

The mob stood, and as usual, several score
   Of those pedestrian Paphians, who abound
In decent London when the daylight's o'er;
   Commodious but immoral, they are found
Useful, like Malthus, in promoting marriage:—
But Juan now is stepping from his carriage 240

31

Into one of the sweetest of hotels,
   Especially for foreigners—and mostly
For those whom favour or whom fortune swells,
   And cannot find a bill's small items costly.
There many an envoy either dwelt or dwells,
   (The den of many a diplomatic lost lie)
Until to some conspicuous square they pass,
And blazon o'er the door their names in brass.

32

Juan, whose was a delicate commission,
   Private, though publicly important, bore 250
No title to point out with due precision
   The exact affair on which he was sent o'er.
'Twas merely known that on a secret mission
   A foreigner of rank had graced our shore,
Young, handsome, and accomplished, who was said
(In whispers) to have turned his Sovereign's head.

33

Some rumour also of some strange adventures
   Had gone before him, and his wars and loves;
And as romantic heads are pretty painters,
   And, above all, an Englishwoman's roves 260
Into the excursive, breaking the indentures
   Of sober reason, wheresoe'er it moves,
He found himself extremely in the fashion,
Which serves our thinking people for a passion.

34

I don't mean that they are passionless, but quite
   The contrary; but then 'tis in the head;

Yet as the consequences are as bright
    As if they acted with the heart instead,
What after all can signify the site
    Of ladies' lucubrations? So they lead   270
In safety to the place for which you start,
What matters if the road be head or heart?

35

Juan presented in the proper place,
    To proper placemen, every Russ credential;
And was received with all the due grimace,
    By those who govern in the mood potential;
Who, seeing a handsome stripling with smooth face,
    Thought (what in state affairs is most essential)
That they as easily might *do* the youngster,
As hawks may pounce upon a woodland songster.   280

36

They erred, as aged men will do; but by
    And by we'll talk of that; and if we don't,
'Twill be because our notion is not high
    Of politicians and their double front,
Who live by lies, yet dare not boldy lie:
    Now what I love in women is, they won't
Or can't do otherwise than lie, but do it
So well, the very truth seems falsehood to it.

37

And, after all, what is a lie? 'Tis but
    The truth in masquerade; and I defy   290
Historians, heroes, lawyers, priests to put
    A fact without some leaven of a lie.
The very shadow of true Truth would shut
    Up annals, revelations, poesy,
And prophecy—except it should be dated
Some years before the incidents relatcd.

38

Praised be all liars and all lies! Who now
    Can tax my mild Muse with misanthropy?

She rings the world's 'Te Deum,' and her brow
 Blushes for those who will not:—but to sigh   300
Is idle; let us like most others bow,
 Kiss hands, feet, any part of Majesty,
After the good example of 'Green Erin,'
Whose Shamrock now seems rather worse for wearing.

39

Don Juan was presented, and his dress
 And mien excited general admiration—
I don't know which was most admired or less:
 One monstrous diamond drew much observation,
Which Catherine in a moment of 'ivresse'
 (In love or brandy's fervent fermentation) 310
Bestowed upon him, as the public learned;
And, to say truth, it had been fairly earned.

40

Besides the Ministers and underlings,
 Who must be courteous to the accredited
Diplomatists of rather wavering kings,
 Until their royal riddle's fully read,
The very clerks—those somewhat dirty springs
 Of office, or the House of Office, fed
By foul corruption into streams,—even they
Were hardly rude enough to earn their pay. 320

41

And insolence no doubt is what they are
 Employed for, since it is their daily labour,
In the dear offices of peace and war;
 And should you doubt, pray ask of your next neighbour,
When for a passport, or some other bar
 To freedom, he applied (a grief and a bore)
If he found not this spawn of tax-born riches,
Like lap-dogs, the least civil sons of b——s.

42

But Juan was received with much 'empressement:'—
 These phrases of refinement I must borrow 330

From our next neighbour's land, where, like a chessman,
   There is a move set down for joy or sorrow
Not only in mere talking, but the press. Man
   In islands is, it seems, downright and thorough,
More than on continents—as if the sea
(See Billingsgate) made even the tongue more free.

43

And yet the British 'Damme's' rather Attic:
   Your Continental oaths are but incontinent,
And turn on things which no Aristocratic
   Spirit would name, and therefore even I won't anent   340
This subject quote; as it would be schismatic
   In politesse, and have a sound affronting in't:—
But 'Damme's' quite ethereal, though too daring—
Platonic blasphemy, the soul of swearing.

44

For downright rudeness, ye may stay at home;
   For true or false politeness (and scarce *that*
Now) you may cross the blue deep and white foam—
   The first the emblem (rarely though) of what
You leave behind—the next of much you come
   To meet. However, 'tis no time to chat   350
On general topics: poems must confine
Themselves to Unity, like this of mine.

45

In the Great World,—which being interpreted
   Meaneth the West or worst end of a city,
And about twice two thousand people bred
   By no means to be very wise or witty,
But to sit up while others lie in bed,
   And look down on the universe with pity,—
Juan, as an inveterate Patrician,
Was well received by persons of condition.   360

46

He was a bachelor, which is a matter
   Of import both to Virgin and to Bride,

The former's hymeneal hopes to flatter;
   And (should she not hold fast by love or pride)
'Tis also of some moment to the latter:
   A rib's a thorn in a wed Gallant's side,
Requires decorum, and is apt to double
The horrid sin—and what's still worse, the trouble.

47

But Juan was a bachelor—of arts,
   And parts, and hearts: he danced and sung, and had   370
An air as sentimental as Mozart's
   Softest of melodies; and could be sad
Or cheerful, without any 'flaws or starts',
   Just at the proper time; and though a lad,
Had seen the world—which is a curious sight,
And very much unlike what people write.

48

Fair virgins blushed upon him; wedded dames
   Bloomed also in less transitory hues;
For both commodities dwell by the Thames,
   The painting and the painted; youth, ceruse,   380
Against his heart preferred their usual claims,
   Such as no gentleman can quite refuse;
Daughters admired his dress, and pious mothers
Enquired his income, and if he had brothers.

49

The milliners who furnish 'drapery Misses'
   Throughout the season, upon speculation
Of payment ere the honeymoon's last kisses
   Have waned into a crescent's coruscation,
Thought such an opportunity as this is,
   Of a rich foreigner's initiation,   390
Not to be overlooked,—and gave such credit,
That future bridegrooms swore, and sighed, and paid it.

50

The Blues, that tender tribe, who sigh o'er sonnets,
   And with the pages of the last Review

Line the interior of their heads or bonnets,
   Advanced in all their azure's highest hue:
They talked bad French of Spanish, and upon its
   Late authors asked him for a hint or two;
And which was softest, Russian or Castilian?
And whether in his travels he saw Ilion?   400

51

Juan, who was a little superficial,
   And not in literature a great Drawcansir,
Examined by this learned and especial
   Jury of matrons, scarce knew what to answer:
His duties warlike, loving, or official,
   His steady application as a dancer,
Had kept him from the brink of Hippocrene,
Which now he found was blue instead of green.

52

However, he replied at hazard, with
   A modest confidence and calm assurance,   410
Which lent his learned lucubrations pith,
   And passed for arguments of good endurance.
That prodigy, Miss Araminta Smith,
   (Who at sixteen translated 'Hercules Furens'
Into as furious English) with her best look,
Set down his sayings in her common-place book.

53

Juan knew several languages—as well
   He might—and brought them up with skill, in time
To save his fame with each accomplished belle,
   Who still regretted that he did not rhyme.   420
There wanted but this requisite to swell
   His qualities (with them) into sublime:
Lady Fitz-Frisky, and Miss Maevia Mannish,
Both longed extremely to be sung in Spanish.

54

However, he did pretty well, and was
   Admitted as an aspirant to all

The Coteries; and, as in Banquo's glass,
   At great assemblies or in parties small,
He saw ten thousand living authors pass,
   That being about their average numeral;   430
Also the eighty 'greatest living poets,'
As every paltry magazine can show *its*.

55

In twice five years the 'greatest living poet,'
   Like to the champion in the fisty ring,
Is called on to support his claim, or show it,
   Although 'tis an imaginary thing.
Even I—albeit I'm sure I did not know it,
   Nor sought of foolscap subjects to be king,—
Was reckoned, a considerable time,
The grand Napoleon of the realms of rhyme.   440

56

But Juan was my Moscow, and Faliero
   My Leipsic, and my Mont Saint Jean seems Cain:
'La Belle Alliance' of dunces down at zero,
   Now that the Lion's fall'n, may rise again:
But I will fall at least as fell my hero;
   Nor reign at all, or as a *monarch* reign;
Or to some lonely isle of Jailors go,
With turncoat Southey for my turnkey Lowe.

57

Sir Walter reigned before me; Moore and Campbell
   Before and after; but now grown more holy,   450
The Muses upon Sion's hill must ramble,
   With poets almost clergymen, or wholly;
And Pegasus hath a psalmodic amble
   Beneath the reverend Cambyses Croly,
Who shoes the glorious animal with stilts,
A modern Ancient Pistol—'by these Hilts!'

58

Still he excels that artificial hard
   Labourer in the same vineyard, though the vine

Yields him but vinegar for his reward,—
   That neutralized dull Dorus of the Nine;   460
That swarthy Sporus, neither man nor bard;
   That ox of verse, who *ploughs* for every line:—
Cambyses' roaring Romans beat at least
The howling Hebrews of Cybele's priest.—

59

Then there's my gentle Euphues; who, they say,
   Sets up for being a sort of *moral me*;
He'll find it rather difficult some day
   To turn out both, or either, it may be.
Some persons think that Coleridge hath the sway;
   And Wordsworth has supporters, two or three;   470
And that deep-mouthed Boeotian, 'Savage Landor,'
Has taken for a swan rogue Southey's gander.

60

John Keats, who was killed off by one critique,
   Just as he really promised something great,
If not intelligible,—without Greek
   Contrived to talk about the Gods of late,
Much as they might have been supposed to speak.
   Poor fellow! His was an untoward fate:—
'Tis strange the mind, that very fiery particle,
Should let itself be snuffed out by an Article.   480

61

The list grows long of live and dead pretenders
   To that which none will gain—or none will know
The Conqueror at least; who, ere time renders
   His last award, will have the long grass grow
Above his burnt-out brain, and sapless cinders.
   If I might augur, I should rate but low
Their chances;—they're too numerous, like the thirty
Mock tyrants, when Rome's annals waxed but dirty.

62

This is the literary *lower* Empire,
   Where the Praetorian bands take up the matter;—   490

A 'dreadful trade,' like his who 'gathers samphire',
    The insolent soldiery to soothe and flatter,
With the same feelings as you'd coax a vampire.
    Now, were I once at home, and in good satire,
I'd try conclusions with those Janizaries,
And show them *what* an intellectual war is.

63

I think I know a trick or two, would turn
    Their flanks;—but it is hardly worth my while
With such small gear to give myself concern:
    Indeed I've not the necessary bile;   500
My natural temper's really aught but stern,
    And even my Muse's worst reproof's a smile;
And then she drops a brief and modern curtsey,
And glides away, assured she never hurts ye.

64

My Juan, whom I left in deadly peril
    Amongst live poets and blue ladies, past
With some small profit through that field so sterile.
    Being tired in time, and neither least nor last
Left it before he had been treated very ill;
    And henceforth found himself more gaily classed   510
Amongst the higher spirits of the day,
The sun's true son, no vapour, but a ray.

65

His morns he passed in business—which dissected,
    Was like all business, a laborious nothing,
That leads to lassitude, the most infected
    And Centaur–Nessus garb of mortal clothing,
And on our sophas makes us lie dejected,
    And talk in tender horrors of our loathing
All kinds of toil, save for our country's good—
Which grows no better, though 'tis time it should.   520

66

His afternoons he passed in visits, luncheons,
    Lounging, and boxing; and the twilight hour

In riding round those vegetable puncheons
   Called 'Parks,' where there is neither fruit nor flower
Enough to gratify a bee's slight munchings;
   But after all it is the only 'bower,'
(In Moore's phrase) where the fashionable fair
Can form a slight acquaintance with fresh air.

67

Then dress, then dinner, then awakes the world!
   Then glare the lamps, then whirl the wheels, then roar   530
Through street and square fast flashing chariots, hurled
   Like harnessed meteors; then along the floor
Chalk mimics painting; then festoons are twirled;
   Then roll the brazen thunders of the door,
Which opens to the thousand happy few
An earthly Paradise of 'Or Molu'.

68

There stands the noble Hostess, nor shall sink
   With the three-thousandth curtsey; there the Waltz,
The only dance which teaches girls to think,
   Makes one in love with its very faults.   540
Saloon, room, hall o'erflow beyond their brink,
   And long the latest of arrivals halts,
'Midst royal dukes and dames condemned to climb,
And gain an inch of staircase at a time.

69

Thrice happy he, who, after a survey
   Of the good company, can win a corner,
A door that's *in*, or boudoir *out* of the way,
   Where he may fix himself, like small 'Jack Horner,'
And let the Babel round run as it may,
   And look on as a mourner, or a scorner,   550
Or an approver, or a mere spectator,
Yawning a little as the night grows later.

70

But this won't do, save by and by; and he
   Who, like Don Juan, takes an active share,

Must steer with care through all that glittering sea
   Of gems and plumes, and pearls and silks, to where
He deems it is his proper place to be;
   Dissolving in the waltz to some soft air,
Or proudlier prancing with mercurial skill
Where Science marshals forth her own quadrille.   560

71

Or, if he dance not, but hath higher views
   Upon an heiress or his neighbour's bride,
Let him take care that that which he pursues
   Is not at once too palpably descried.
Full many an eager gentleman oft rues
   His haste: impatience is a blundering guide
Amongst a people famous for reflection,
Who like to play the fool with circumspection.

72

But, if you can contrive, get next at supper;
   Or, if forestalled, get opposite and ogle:—   570
Oh, ye ambrosial moments! always upper
   In mind, a sort of sentimental bogle,
Which sits for ever upon Memory's crupper,
   The ghost of vanished pleasures once in vogue! Ill
Can tender souls relate the rise and fall
Of hopes and fears which shake a single ball.

73

But these precautionary hints can touch
   Only the common run, who must pursue,
And watch, and ward; whose plans a word too much
   Or little overturns; and not the few   580
Or many (for the number's sometimes such)
   Whom a good mien, especially if new,
Or fame, or name, for wit, war, sense, or nonsense,
Permits whate'er they please, or *did* not long since.

74

Our hero, as a hero, young and handsome,
   Noble, rich, celebrated, and a stranger,

Like other slaves of course must pay his ransom
  Before he can escape from so much danger
As will environ a conspicuous man. Some
  Talk about poetry, and 'rack and manger',   590
And ugliness, disease, as toil and trouble,—
I wish they knew the life of a young noble.

75

They are young, but know not youth—it is anticipated;
  Handsome but wasted, rich without a sou;
Their vigour in a thousand arms is dissipated;
  Their cash comes *from*, their wealth goes *to* a Jew;
Both senates see their nightly votes participated
  Between the tyrant's and the tribunes' crew;
And having voted, dined, drank, gamed, and whored,
The family vault receives another lord.   600

76

'Where is the world,' cries Young, 'at *eighty*? Where
  The world in which a man was born?' Alas!
Where is the world of *eight* years past? *'Twas there*—
  I look for it—'tis gone, a Globe of Glass!
Cracked, shivered, vanished, scarcely gazed on, ere
  A silent change dissolves the glittering mass.
Statesmen, chiefs, orators, queens, patriots, kings,
And dandies, all are gone on the wind's wings.

77

Where is Napoleon the Grand? God knows:
  Where little Castlereagh? The devil can tell: 610
Where Grattan, Curran, Sheridan, all those
  Who bound the bar or senate in their spell?
Where is the unhappy Queen, with all her woes?
  And where the Daughter, whom the Isles loved well?
Where are those martyred Saints the Five per Cents?
And where—oh where the devil are the Rents!

78

Where's Brummell? Dished. Where's Long Pole
  Wellesley? Diddled.

Where's Whitbread? Romilly? Where's George the Third?
Where is his will? (That's not so soon unriddled.)
    And where is 'Fum' the Fourth, our 'royal bird'?   620
Gone down it seems to Scotland, to be fiddled
    Unto by Sawney's violin, we have heard:
'Caw me, caw thee'—for six months hath been hatching
This scene of royal itch and loyal scratching.

79

Where is Lord This? And where my Lady That?
    The Honourable Mistresses and Misses?
Some laid aside like an old opera hat,
    Married, unmarried, and remarried: (this is
An evolution oft performed of late).
    Where are the Dublin shouts—and London hisses?   630
Where are the Grenvilles? Turned as usual. Where
My friends the Whigs? Exactly where they were.

80

Where are the Lady Carolines and Franceses?
    Divorced or doing thereanent. Ye annals
So brilliant, where the list of routs and dances is,—
    Thou Morning Post, sole record of the panels
Broken in carriages, and all the phantasies
    Of fashion,—say what streams now fill those channels?
Some die, some fly, some languish on the Continent,
Because the times have hardly left them *one* tenant.   640

81

Some who once set their caps at cautious Dukes,
    Have taken up at length with younger brothers:
Some heiresses have bit at sharpers' hooks;
    Some maids have been made wives, some merely mothers;
Others have lost their fresh and fairy looks:
    In short, the list of alterations bothers:
There's little strange in this, but something strange is
The unusual quickness of these common changes.

82

Talk not of seventy years as age! in seven
   I have seen more changes, down from monarchs to   650
The humblest individual under heaven,
   Than might suffice a moderate century through.
I knew that nought was lasting, but now even
   Change grows too changeable, without being new:
Nought's permanent among the human race,
Except the Whigs *not* getting into place.

83

I have seen Napoleon, who seemed quite a Jupiter,
   Shrink to a Saturn. I have seen a Duke
(No matter which) turn politician stupider,
   If that can well be, than his wooden look.   660
But it is time that I should hoist my 'blue Peter',
   And sail for a new theme:—I have seen—and shook
To see it—the King hissed, and then carest;
And don't pretend to settle which was best.

84

I have seen the landholder's without a rap—
   I have seen Joanna Southcote—I have seen
The House of Commons turned to a tax-trap—
   I have seen that sad affair of the late Queen—
I have seen crowns worn instead of a fool's-cap—
   I have seen a Congress doing all that's mean—   670
I have seen some nations like o'erloaded asses
Kick off their burthens—meaning the high classes.

85

I have seen small poets, and great prosers, and
   Interminable—*not eternal*—speakers—
I have seen the Funds at war with house and land—
   I've seen the Country Gentlemen turn squeakers—
I've seen the people ridden o'er like sand
   By slaves on horseback—I have seen malt liquors
Exchanged for 'thin potations' by John Bull—
I have seen John half detect himself a fool.—   680

86

But 'Carpe diem,' Juan, 'Carpe, carpe!'
　　To-morrow sees another race as gay
And transient, and devoured by the same harpy.
　　'Life's a poor player,'—then 'play out the play,
Ye villains!' and above all keep a sharp eye
　　Much less on what you do than what you say:
Be hypocritical, be cautious, be
Not what you *seem*, but always what you *see*.

87

But how shall I relate in other Cantos
　　Of what befell our hero in the land,   690
Which 'tis the common cry and lie to vaunt as
　　A moral country? But I hold my hand—
For I disdain to write an Atalantis;
　　But 'tis as well at once to understand,
You are *not* a moral people, and you know it
Without the aid of too sincere a poet.

88

What Juan saw and underwent, shall be
　　My topic, with of course the due restriction
Which is required by proper courtesy;
　　And recollect the work is only fiction,   700
And that I sing of neither mine nor me,
　　Though every scribe, in some slight turn of diction,
Will hint allusions never *meant*. Ne'er doubt
This—when I speak, I *don't hint*, but *speak out*.

89

Whether he married with the third or fourth
　　Offspring of some sage, husband-hunting Countess,
Or whether with some virgin of more worth
　　(I mean in Fortune's matrimonial bounties)
He took to regularly peopling Earth,
　　Of which your lawful awful wedlock fount is,—   710
Or whether he was taken in for damages,
For being too excursive in his homages,—

90

Is yet within the unread events of time.
    Thus far, go forth, thou Lay! which I will back
Against the same given quantity of rhyme,
    For being as much the subject of attack
As ever yet was any work sublime,
    By those who love to say that white is black.
So much the better!—I may stand alone,
And would not change my free thoughts for a throne.   720

[1823]

from *Canto XIV*

1

If from great Nature's or our own abyss
    Of thought, we could but snatch a certainty,
Perhaps mankind might find the path they miss—
    But then 'twould spoil much good philosophy.
One system eats another up, and this
    Much as old Saturn ate his progeny;
For when his pious consort gave him stones
In lieu of sons, of these he made no bones.

2

But System doth reverse the Titan's breakfast
    And eats her parents, albeit the digestion   10
Is difficult. Pray tell me, can you make fast,
    After due search, your faith to any question?
Look back o'er ages, ere unto the stake fast
    You bind yourself, and call some mode the best one.
Nothing more true than *not* to trust your senses;
And yet what are your other evidences?

3

For me, I know nought; nothing I deny,
    Admit, reject, contemn; and what know *you*,

Except perhaps that you were born to die?
  And both may after all turn out untrue.
An age may come, Font of Eternity,   20
  When nothing shall be either old or new.
Death, so call'd, is a thing which makes men weep,
And yet a third of life is pass'd in sleep.

4

A sleep without dreams, after a rough day
  Of toil, is what we covet most; and yet
How clay shrinks back from more quiescent clay!
  The very Suicide that pays his debt
At once without instalments (an old way
  Of paying debts, which creditors regret)   30
Lets out impatiently his rushing breath,
Less from disgust of life than dread of death.

5

'Tis round him, near him, here, there, every where;
  And there's a courage which grows out of fear,
Perhaps of all most desperate, which will dare
  The worst to *know* it:—when the mountains rear
Their peaks beneath your human foot, and there
  You look down o'er the precipice, and drear
The gulf of rock yawns,—you can't gaze a minute
Without an awful wish to plunge within it.   40

6

'Tis true, you don't—but, pale and struck with terror,
  Retire: but look into your past impression!
And you will find, though shuddering at the mirror
  Of your own thoughts, in all their self confession,
The lurking bias, be it truth or error,
  To the *unknown*; a secret prepossession,
To plunge with all your fears—but where? You know not,
And that's the reason why you do—or do not.

7

But what's this to the purpose? you will say.
  Gent. Reader, nothing; a mere speculation,   50

For which my sole excuse is—'tis my way,
   Sometimes *with* and sometimes without occasion
I write what's uppermost, without delay;
   This narrative is not meant for narration,
But a mere airy and fantastic basis,
To build up common things with common places.

8

You know, or don't know, that great Bacon saith,
   'Fling up a straw, 'twill show the way the wind blows;'
And such a straw, borne on by human breath,
   Is Poesy, according as the mind glows;   60
A paper kite, which flies 'twixt life and death,
   A shadow which the onward Soul behind throws:
And mine's a bubble not blown up for praise,
But just to play with, as an infant plays.

9

The world is all before me, or behind;
   For I have seen a portion of that same,
And quite enough for me to keep in mind;—
   Of passions too, I have proved enough to blame,
To the great pleasure of our friends, mankind,
   Who like to mix some slight alloy with fame: 70
For I was rather famous in my time,
Until I fairly knock'd it up with rhyme.

10

I have brought this world about my ears, and eke
   The other; that's to say, the Clergy—who
Upon my head have bid their thunders break
   In pious libels by no means a few.
And yet I can't help scribbling once a week,
   Tiring old readers, nor discovering new.
In youth I wrote, because my mind was full,
And now because I feel it growing dull.   80

11

But 'why then publish?'—There are no rewards
   Of fame or profit, when the world grows weary.

I ask in turn,—why do you play at cards?
    Why drink? Why read?—To make some hour less dreary.
It occupies me to turn back regards
    On what I've seen or ponder'd, sad or cheery;
And what I write I cast upon the stream,
To swim or sink—I have had at least my dream.

12

I think that were I *certain* of success,
    I hardly could compose another line: 90
So long I've battled either more or less,
    That no defeat can drive me from the Nine.
This feeling 'tis not easy to express,
    And yet 'tis not affected, I opine.
In play, there are two pleasures for your choosing—
The one is winning, and the other losing.

13

Besides, my Muse by no means deals in fiction:
    She gathers a repertory of facts,
Of course with some reserve and slight restriction,
    But mostly sings of human things and acts—   100
And that's one cause she meets with contradiction;
    For too much truth, at first sight, ne'er attracts;
And were her object only what's call'd glory,
With more ease too she'd tell a different story.

14

Love, war, a tempest—surely there's variety;
    Also a seasoning slight of lucubration;
A bird's-eye view too of that wild, Society;
    A slight glance thrown on men of every station.
If you have nought else, here's at least satiety
    Both in performance and in preparation;   110
And though these lines should only line portmanteaus,
Trade will be all the better for these Cantos.

15

The portion of this world which I at present
    Have taken up to fill the following sermon,

Is one of which there's no description recent:
    The reason why, is easy to determine:
Although it seems both prominent and pleasant,
    There is a sameness in its gems and ermine,
A dull and family likeness through all ages,
Of no great promise for poetic pages.   120

16

With much to excite, there's little to exalt;
    Nothing that speaks to all men and all times;
A sort of varnish over every fault;
    A kind of common-place, even in their crimes:
Factitious passions, wit without much salt,
    A want of that true nature which sublimes
Whate'er it shows with truth; a smooth monotony
Of character, in those at least who have got any.

17

Sometimes indeed, like soldiers off parade,
    They break their ranks and gladly leave the drill;   130
But then the roll-call draws them back afraid,
    And they must be or seem what they were: still
Doubtless it is a brilliant masquerade;
    But when of the first sight you have had your fill,
It palls—at least it did so upon me,
This Paradise of Pleasure and *Ennui*.

18

When we have made our love, and gamed our gaming,
    Drest, voted, shone, and, may be, something more;
With dandies dined; heard senators declaiming;
    Seen beauties brought to market by the score;   140
Sad rakes to sadder husbands chastely taming;
    There's little left but to be bored or bore.
Witness those '*ci-devant jeunes hommes*' who stem
The stream, nor leave the world which leaveth them.

19

'Tis said—indeed a general complaint—
    That no one has succeeded in describing

The *Monde*, exactly as they ought to paint.
  Some say, that Authors only snatch, by bribing
The porter, some slight scandals strange and quaint,
  To furnish matter for their moral gibing;   150
And that their books have but one style in common—
My lady's prattle, filter'd through her woman.

20

But this can't well be true just now; for writers
  Are grown of the *Beau Monde* a part potential:
I've seen them balance even the scale with fighters,
  Especially when young, for that's essential.
Why do their sketches fail them as inditers
  Of what they deem themselves most consequential—
The *real* portrait of the highest tribe?
'Tis that, in fact, there's little to describe.   160

21

'*Haud ignara loquor:*' these are *Nugae*, '*quarum*
  Pars parva *fui*,' but still Art and part.
Now I could much more easily sketch a harem,
  A battle, wreck, or history of the heart,
Than these things; and besides, I wish to spare 'em,
  For reasons which I choose to keep apart.
'*Vetabo Cereris sacrum qui vulgaret*'—
Which means that vulgar people must not share it.

22

And therefore what I throw off is ideal—
  Lower'd, leaven'd, like a history of Freemasons;   170
Which bears the same relation to the real,
  As Captain Parry's voyage may do to Jason's.
The grand Arcanum's not for me to see all;
  My music has some mystic diapasons;
And there is much which could not be appreciated
In any manner by the uninitiated.

[1823]

from *Canto XV*

[*Dinner at The Amundeville Estate*]

40

But Adeline determined Juan's wedding
  In her own mind, and that's enough for woman.
But then, with whom? There was the sage Miss Reading,
  Miss Raw, Miss Flaw, Miss Showman, and Miss
    Knowman,
And the two fair co-heiresses Giltbedding.
  She deemed his merits something more than common:
All these were unobjectionable matches,
And might go on, if well wound up, like watches.

41

There was Miss Millpond, smooth as summer's sea,
  That usual paragon, an only daughter,   10
Who seem'd the cream of equanimity,
  Till skimm'd—and then there was some milk and water,
With a slight shade of Blue too it might be,
  Beneath the surface; but what did it matter?
Love's riotous, but marriage should have quiet,
And being consumptive, live on a milk diet.

42

And then there was the Miss Audacia Shoestring,
  A dashing demoiselle of good estate,
Whose heart was fix'd upon a star or bluestring;
  But whether English Dukes grew rare of late,   20
Or that she had not harp'd upon the true string,
  By which such sirens can attract our great,
She took up with some foreign younger brother,
A Russ or Turk—the one's as good as t'other.

43

And then there was—but why should I go on,
  Unless the ladies should go off?—there was

Indeed a certain fair and fairy one,
   Of the best class, and better than her class,—
Aurora Raby, a young star who shone
   O'er life, too sweet an image for such glass,   30
A lovely being, scarcely form'd or moulded,
A Rose with all its sweetest leaves yet folded;

44

Rich, noble, but an orphan; left an only
   Child to the care of guardians good and kind;
But still her aspect had an air so lonely!
   Blood is not water; and where shall we find
Feelings of youth like those which overthrown lie
   By death, when we are left, alas! behind,
To feel, in friendless palaces, a home
Is wanting, and our best ties in the tomb?   40

45

Early in years, and yet more infantine
   In figure, she had something of sublime
In eyes which sadly shone, as seraphs' shine.
   All youth—but with an aspect beyond time;
Radiant and grave—as pitying man's decline;
   Mournful—but mournful of another's crime,
She look'd as if she sat by Eden's door,
And grieved for those who could return no more.

46

She was a Catholic too, sincere, austere,
   A far as her own gentle heart allow'd,   50
And deem'd that fallen worship far more dear
   Perhaps because 'twas fallen: her sires were proud
Of deeds and days when they had fill'd the ear
   Of nations, and had never bent or bow'd
To novel power; and as she was the last,
She held their old faith and old feelings fast.

47

She gazed upon a world she scarcely knew
   As seeking not to know it; silent, lone,

As grows a flower, thus quietly she grew,
   And kept her heart serene within its zone.   60
There was awe in the homage which she drew;
   Her spirit seem'd as seated on a throne
Apart from the surrounding world, and strong
In its own strength—most strange in one so young!

48

Now it so happen'd, in the catalogue
   Of Adeline, Aurora was omitted,
Although her birth and wealth had given her vogue
   Beyond the charmers we have already cited;
Her beauty also seem'd to form no clog
   Against her being mention'd as well fitted,   70
By many virtues, to be worth the trouble
Of single gentlemen who would be double.

49

And this omission, like that of the bust
   Of Brutus at the pageant of Tiberius,
Made Juan wonder, as no doubt he must.
   This he express'd half smiling and half serious;
When Adeline replied with some disgust,
   And with an air, to say the least, impervious,
She marvell'd 'what he saw in such a baby
As that prim, silent, cold Aurora Raby?'   80

50

Juan rejoined—'She was a Catholic,
   And therefore fittest, as of his persuasion;
Since he was sure his mother would fall sick,
   And the Pope thunder excommunication,
If—' But here Adeline, who seem'd to pique
   Herself extremely on the inoculation
Of others with her own opinions, stated—
As usual—the same reason which she late did.

51

And wherefore not? A reasonable reason,
   If good, is none the worst for repetition;   90

If bad, the best way's certainly to teaze on
    And amplify: you lose much by concision,
Whereas insisting in or out of season
    Convinces all men, even a politician;
Or—what is just the same—it wearies out.
So the end's gain'd, what signifies the route?

                        52

Why Adeline had this slight prejudice—
    For prejudice it was—against a creature
As pure as sanctity itself from vice,
    With all the added charm of form and feature,   100
For me appears a question far too nice,
    Since Adeline was liberal by Nature;
But Nature's Nature, and has more caprices
Than I have time, or will, to take to pieces.

                        53

Perhaps she did not like the quiet way
    With which Aurora on those baubles look'd,
Which charm most people in their earlier day:
    For there are few things by mankind less brook'd,
And womankind too, if we so may say,
    Than finding thus their genius stand rebuked,   110
Like 'Anthony's by Caesar,' by the few
Who look upon them as they ought to do.

                        54

It was not envy—Adeline had none;
    Her place was far beyond it, and her mind.
It was not scorn—which could not light on one
    Whose greatest *fault* was leaving few to find.
It was not jealousy, I think: but shun
    Following the 'Ignes Fatui' of mankind.
It was not—but 'tis easier far, alas!
To say what it was not, than what it was.   120

                        55

Little Aurora deem'd she was the theme
    Of such discussion. She was there a guest,

A beauteous ripple of the brilliant stream
  Of rank and youth, though purer than the rest,
Which flow'd on for a moment in the beam
  Time sheds a moment o'er each sparkling crest.
Had she known this, she would have calmly smiled—
She had so much, or little, of the child.

56

The dashing and proud air of Adeline
  Imposed not upon her: she saw her blaze   130
Much as she would have seen a glowworm shine,
  Then turn'd unto the stars for loftier rays.
Juan was something she could not divine,
  Being no Sibyl in the new world's ways;
Yet she was nothing dazzled by the meteor,
Because she did not pin her faith on feature.

57

His fame too,—for he had that kind of fame
  Which sometimes plays the deuce with womankind,
A heterogeneous mass of glorious blame,
  Half virtues and whole vices being combined;   140
Faults which attract because they are not tame;
  Follies trick'd out so brightly that they blind:—
These seals upon her wax made no impression,
Such was her coldness or her self-possession.

58

Juan knew nought of such a character—
  High, yet resembling not his lost Haidée;
Yet each was radiant in her proper sphere:
  The Island girl, bred up by the lone sea,
More warm, as lovely, and not less sincere,
  Was Nature's all: Aurora could not be   150
Nor would be thus;—the difference in them
Was such as lies between a flower and gem.

59

Having wound up with this sublime comparison,
  Methinks we may proceed upon our narrative,

And, as my friend Scott says, 'I sound my Warison;'
   Scott, the superlative of my comparative—
Scott, who can paint your Christian knight or Saracen,
   Serf, Lord, Man, with such skill as none would share it if
There had not been one Shakespeare and Voltaire,
Of one or both of whom he seems the heir.   160

60

I say, in my slight way I may proceed
   To play upon the surface of Humanity.
I write the world, nor care if the world read,
   At least for this I cannot spare its vanity.
My Muse hath bred, and still perhaps may breed
   More foes by this same scroll: when I began it, I
Thought that it might turn out so—*now* I *know* it,
But still I am, or was, a pretty poet.

61

The conference or congress (for it ended
   As congresses of late do) of the Lady   170
Adeline and Don Juan rather blended
   Some acids with the sweets—for she was heady;
But, ere the matter could be marr'd or mended,
   The silvery bell rung, not for 'dinner ready,'
But for that hour, called *half-hour*, given to dress,
Though ladies' robes seem scant enough for less.

62

Great things were now to be achieved at table,
   With massy plate for armour, knives and forks
For weapons; but what Muse since Homer's able
   (His feasts are not the worst part of his works)   180
To draw up in array a single day-bill
   Of modern dinners? where more mystery lurks
In soups or sauces, or a sole ragoût,
Than witches, b—ches, or physicians brew.

63

There was a goodly 'soupe à la *bonne femme*,'
   Though God knows whence it came from; there was too

A turbot for relief of those who cram,
   Relieved with dindon a la Périgueux;
There also was—the sinner that I am!
   How shall I get this gourmand stanza through?—   190
Soupe à la Beauveau, whose relief was Dory,
Relieved itself by pork, for greater glory.

64

But I must crowd all into one grand mess
   Or mass; for should I stretch into detail,
My Muse would run much more into excess,
   Than when some squeamish people deem her frail.
But though a 'bonne vivante,' I must confess
   Her stomach's not her peccant part: this tale
However doth require some slight refection,
Just to relieve her spirits from dejection.   200

65

Fowls à la Condé, slices eke of salmon,
   With sauces Genevoises, and haunch of venison;
Wines too which might again have slain young Ammon—
   A man like whom I hope we shan't see many soon;
They also set a glazed Westphalian ham on,
   Whereon Apicius would bestow his benison;
And then there was Champagne with foaming whirls,
As white as Cleopatra's melted pearls.

66

Then there was God knows what 'à l'Allemande,'
   'A l'Espagnole,' 'timballe,' and 'Salpicon'—   210
With things I can't withstand or understand,
   Though swallow'd with much zest upon the whole;
And 'entremets' to piddle with at hand,
   Gently to lull down the subsiding soul;
While great Lucullus' *Robe triumphal* muffles—
(There's Fame)—young Partridge' fillets, deck'd with truffles.

67

What are the *fillets* on the victor's brow
   To these? They are rags or dust. Where is the arch

Which nodded to the nation's spoils below?
  Where the triumphal chariots' haughty march?   220
Gone to where victories must like dinners go.
  Further I shall not follow the research:
But oh! ye modern heroes with your cartridges,
When will your names lend lustre even to partridges?

68

Those truffles too are no bad accessaries,
  Followed by 'Petits puits d'Amour'—a dish
Of which perhaps the cookery rather varies,
  So every one may dress it to his wish,
According to the best of dictionaries,
  Which encyclopedize both flesh and fish;   230
But even sans 'confitures,' it no less true is,
There's pretty picking in those 'petits puits.'

69

The mind is lost in mighty contemplation
  Of intellect expended on two courses;
And indigestion's grand multiplication
  Requires arithmetic beyond my forces.
Who would suppose, from Adam's simple ration,
  That cookery could have call'd forth such resources,
As form a science and a nomenclature
From out the commonest demands of nature?   240

70

The glasses jingled, and the palates tingled;
  The diners of celebrity dined well;
The ladies with more moderation mingled
  In the feast, pecking less than I can tell;
Also the younger men too; for a springald
  Can't like ripe age in gourmandise excel,
But thinks less of good eating than the whisper
(When seated next him) of some pretty lisper.

71

Alas! I must leave undescribed the gibier,
  The salmi, the consommé, the purée,   250

All which I used to make my rhymes run glibber
   Than could roast beef in our rough John Bull way:
I must not introduce even a spare rib here,
   'Bubble and squeak' would spoil my liquid lay;
But I have dined, and must forego, alas!
The chaste description even of a 'Becasse,'

72

And fruits, and ice, and all that art refines
   From nature for the service of the goût,—
Taste or the *gout*,—pronounce it as inclines
   Your stomach! Ere you dine, the French will do;   260
But *after*, there are sometimes certain signs
   Which prove plain English truer of the two.
Has ever *had* the *gout*? I have not had it—
But I may have, and you too, Reader, dread it.

73

The simple olives, best allies of wine,
   Must I pass over in my bill of fare?
I must, although a favourite 'plat' of mine
   In Spain, and Lucca, Athens, every where:
On them and bread 'twas oft my luck to dine,
   The grass my table-cloth, in open air,   270
On Sunium or Hymettus, like Diogenes,
Of whom half my philosophy the progeny is.

74

Amidst this tumult of fish, flesh, and fowl,
   And vegetables, all in masquerade,
The guests were placed according to their roll,
   But various as the various meats display'd:
Don Juan sat next an 'à l'Espagnole'—
   No damsel, but a dish, as hath been said;
But so far like a lady, that 'twas drest
Superbly, and contained a world of zest.   280

75

By some odd chance too he was placed between
   Aurora and the Lady Adeline—

A situation difficult, I ween,
  For man therein, with eyes and heart, to dine.
Also the conference which we have seen
  Was not such as to encourage him to shine;
For Adeline, addressing few words to him,
With two transcendant eyes seemed to look through him.

76

I sometimes almost think that eyes have ears:
  This much is sure, that, out of earshot, things   290
Are somehow echoed to the pretty dears,
  Of which I can't tell whence their knowledge springs;
Like that same mystic music of the spheres,
  Which no one hears so loudly though it rings.
'Tis wonderful how oft the sex have heard
Long dialogues which pass'd without a word!

77

Aurora state with that indifference
  Which piques a preux Chevalier—as it ought:
Of all offences that's the worst offence,
  Which seems to hint you are not worth a thought.   300
Now Juan, though no coxcomb in pretence,
  Was not exactly pleased to be so caught:
Like a good ship entangled among ice,
And after so much excellent advice.

78

To his gay nothings, nothing was replied,
  Or something which was nothing, as urbanity
Required. Aurora scarcely look'd aside,
  Nor even smiled enough for any vanity.
The devil was in the girl! Could it be pride?
  Or modesty, or absence, or inanity?   310
Heaven knows! But Adeline's malicious eyes
Sparkled with her successful prophecies,

79

And look'd as much as if to say, 'I said it;'—
  A kind of triumph I'll not recommend,

Because it sometimes, as I've seen or read it,
  Both in the case of lover and of friend,
Will pique a gentleman, for his own credit,
  To bring what was a jest to a serious end:
For all men prophesy what *is* or *was*,
And hate those who won't let them come to pass.   320

80

Juan was drawn thus into some attentions,
  Slight but select, and just enough to express,
To females of perspicuous comprehensions,
  That he would rather make them more than less.
Aurora at the last (so history mentions,
  Though probably much less a fact than guess)
So far relax'd her thoughts from their sweet prison,
As once or twice to smile, if not to listen.

81

From answering, she began to question: this
  With her was rare; and Adeline, who as yet   330
Thought her predictions went not much amiss,
  Began to dread she'd thaw to a coquette—
So very difficult, they say, it is
  To keep extremes from meeting, when once set
In motion; but she here too much refined—
Aurora's spirit was not of that kind.

82

But Juan had a sort of winning way,
  A proud humility, if such there be,
Which show'd such deference to what females say,
  As if each charming word were a decree.   340
His tact too temper'd him from grave to gay,
  And taught him when to be reserved or free:
He had the art of drawing people out,
Without their seeing what he was about.

83

Aurora, who in her indifference
  Confounded him in common with the crowd

Of flutterers, though she deem'd he had more sense
  Than whispering foplings, or than witlings loud,—
Commenced (from such slight things will great commence)
  To feel that flattery which attracts the proud   350
Rather by deference than compliment,
And wins even by a delicate dissent.

84

And then he had good looks;—that point was carried
  Nem. con. amongst the women, which I grieve
To say leads oft to *crim. con.* with the married—
  A case which to the Juries we may leave,
Since with digressions we too long have tarried.
  Now though we know of old that looks deceive,
And always have done, somehow these good looks
Make more impression than the best of books.   360

85

Aurora, who look'd more on books than faces,
  Was very young, although so very sage,
Admiring more Minerva than the Graces,
  Especially upon a printed page.
But Virtue's self, with all her tightest laces,
  Has not the natural stays of strict old age;
And Socrates, that model of all duty,
Own'd to a penchant, though discreet, for beauty.

86

And girls of sixteen are thus far Socratic,
  But innocently so, as Socrates: 370
And really, if the Sage sublime and Attic
  At seventy years had phantasies like these,
Which Plato in his dialogues dramatic
  Has shown, I know not why they should displease
In virgins—always in a modest way,
Observe; for that with me's a 'sine quâ.'

87

Also observe, that like the great Lord Coke,
  (See Littleton) whene'er I have expressed

Opinions two, which at first sight may look
   Twin opposites, the second is the best.   380
Perhaps I have a third too in a nook,
   Or none at all—which seems a sorry jest;
But if a writer should be quite consistent,
How could he possibly show things existent?

88

If people contradict themselves, can I
   Help contradicting them, and every body,
Even my veracious self?—But that's a lie;
   I never did so, never will—how should I?
He who doubts all things, nothing can deny;
   Truth's fountains may be clear—her streams are muddy, 390
And cut through such canals of contradiction,
That she must often navigate o'er fiction.

89

Apologue, fable, poesy, and parable,
   Are false, but may be render'd also true
By those who sow them in a land that's arable.
   'Tis wonderful what fable will not do!
'Tis said it makes reality more bearable:
   But what's reality? Who has its clue?
Philosophy? No; she too much rejects.
Religion? *Yes*; but which of all her sects?   400

90

Some millions must be wrong, that's pretty clear:
   Perhaps it may turn out that all were right.
God help us! Since we have need on our career
   To keep our holy beacons always bright,
'Tis time that some new Prophet should appear,
   Or old indulge man with a second sight.
Opinions wear out in some thousand years,
Without a small refreshment from the spheres.

91

But here again, why will I thus entangle
   Myself with metaphysics? None can hate   410

So much as I do any kind of wrangle;
   And yet, such is my folly, or my fate,
I always knock my head against some angle
   About the present, past, or future state:
Yet I wish well to Trojan and to Tyrian,
For I was bred a moderate Presbyterian.

                        [1824]

Francesca of Rimini

Translation from the Inferno of Dante,
Canto 5.

The reader is requested to consider the following version as an attempt to
render *verse* for *verse* the episode in the same metre. Where the same
English word appears to be repeated too frequently, he will generally find
the corresponding repetition in the Italian; I have sacrificed all ornament
to fidelity.

'The Land where I was born sits by the seas,
   Upon that shore to which the Po descends
   With all his followers in search of peace.
Love, which the gentle heart soon apprehends,
   Seized him for the fair person which was ta'en
   From me, and me even yet the mode offends.
Love, who to none beloved to love again
   Remits, seized me with wish to please so strong
   That, as thou seest, yet, yet it doth remain.
Love to one death conducted us along: 10
   But Caina waits for him our life who ended.'
   These were the accents utter'd by her tongue.
Since I first listened to these souls offended
   I bow'd my visage, and so kept it till
   'What think'st thou?' said the bard—then I unbended
And recommenced, 'Alas! unto such ill
   How many sweet thoughts, what strong ecstacies,
   Led these their evil fortune to fulfill!'
And then I turned unto their side my eyes,
   And said, 'Francesca, thy sad destinies   20

Have made me sorrow till the tears arise.
But tell me, in the season of sweet sighs
   By what, and how thy love to passion rose
   So as his dim desires to recognize?'
Then she to me—'The greatest of all woes
   Is to recal to mind our happy days
   In misery, and that thy teacher knows.
But if to learn our passion's first root preys
   Upon thy spirit with such sympathy,
   I will relate as he who weeps, and says.   30
We read one day for pastime, seated nigh,
   Of Lancelot, how love enchain'd him too;
   We were alone, quite unsuspiciously.
But oft our eyes met, and our cheeks in hue
   All o'er discolour'd by that reading were;
   But one point only wholly us o'erthrew.
When we read the long-sighed-for smile of her
   To be thus kiss'd by such a fervent lover,
   He, who from me can be divided ne'er,
Kiss'd my mouth, trembling in the act all over—   40
   Accursed was the book, and he who wrote;
   That day no further leaf we did uncover.'
While thus one spirit told us of their lot
   The other wept so, that, with pity's thralls,
   I swoon'd, as if by death I had been smote,
And fell down even as a dead body falls.

[1820]

from *Cain* Act II scene 2

CAIN.   Haughty spirit!
  Thou speak'st it proudly; but thyself, though proud,
  Hast a superior.
LUCIFER.   No! by heaven, which He
  Holds, and the abyss, and the immensity
  Of worlds and life, which I hold with him—No!
  I have a victor—true; but no superior.
  Homage he has from all—but none from me:

I battle it against him, as I battled
In highest heaven. Through all eternity,
And the unfathomable gulfs of Hades,   10
And the interminable realms of space,
And the infinity of endless ages,
All, all, will I dispute! And world by world,
And star by star, and universe by universe
Shall tremble in the balance, till the great
Conflict shall cease, if ever it shall cease,
Which it ne'er shall, till he or I be quench'd!
And what can quench our immortality,
Or mutual and irrevocable hate?
He as a conqueror will call the conquer'd   20
Evil; but what will be the *good* he gives?
Were I the victor, *his* works would be deem'd
The only evil ones. And you, ye new
And scarce-born mortals, what have been his gifts
To you already in your little world?
CAIN. But few; and some of those but bitter.
LUCIFER.   Back
  With me, then, to thine earth, and try the rest
Of his celestial boons to ye and yours.
Evil and good are things in their own essence,
And not made good or evil by the giver;   30
But if he gives you good—so call him; if
Evil springs from *him*, do not name it *mine*,
Till ye know better its true fount; and judge
Not by words, though of spirits, but the fruits
Of your existence, such as it must be.
One good gift has the fatal apple given—
Your *reason*:—let it not be over-sway'd
By tyrannous threats to force you into faith
'Gainst all external sense and inward feeling:
Think and endure,—and form an inner world   40
In your own bosom—where the outward fails;
So shall you nearer be the spiritual
Nature, and war triumphant with your own.

                       [They disappear
                        [1821]

[*Thoughts on Freedom*]

They only can feel freedom truly who
Have worn long chains—the healthy feel not health
In all its glow—in all its glory of
Full veins and flushing cheeks and bounding pulses,
Till they have known the interregnum of
Some malady that links them to their beds
In some wide—common—feverish hospital
Where all are tended—and none cared for, left
To public nurses, paid for pity, till
They die—or go forth cured, but without kindness.

[1823]

On This Day I Complete My Thirty-Sixth Year

Messalonghi. January 22nd, 1824.

'Tis time this heart should be unmoved,
  Since others it hath ceased to move:
Yet though I cannot be beloved,
            Still let me love!

My days are in the yellow leaf;
  The flowers and fruits of Love are gone;
The worm—the canker, and the grief
            Are mine alone!

The fire that on my bosom preys
  Is lone as some Volcanic Isle;   10
No torch is kindled at its blaze
            A funeral pile!

The hope, the fear, the jealous care,
  The exalted portion of the pain
And power of Love I cannot share,
            But wear the chain.

But 'tis not *thus*—and 'tis not *here*
  Such thoughts should shake my Soul, nor *now*
Where Glory decks the hero's bier
                Or binds his brow.   20

The Sword, the Banner, and the Field,
  Glory and Greece around us see!
The Spartan borne upon his shield
                Was not more free!

Awake (not Greece—she *is* awake!)
  Awake, my Spirit! think through *whom*
Thy life-blood tracks its parent lake
                And then strike home!

Tread those reviving passions down
  Unworthy Manhood—unto thee
Indifferent should the smile or frown   30
                Of Beauty be.

If thou regret'st thy Youth, *why live?*
  The land of honourable Death
Is here:—up to the Field, and give
                Away thy Breath!

Seek out—less often sought than found—
  A Soldier's Grave, for thee the best;
Then look around, and choose thy Ground,
                And take thy Rest!   40

Notes

1 *A Fragment*. From Byron's first book, *Fugitive Pieces* (1806); an Ossianic imitation.

Damaetas. Published in *Hours of Idleness* (1807). In an unpublished manuscript Byron titled this poem 'My Character'; Damaetas is a name from the pastoral world of Theocritus.

l. 1. i.e. not yet 21 years of age.

2 *Written Beneath a Picture*. Published with *Childe Harold's Pilgrimage. A Romaunt* (1812). Possibly written in memory of John Edleston, the Cambridge choirboy, dear to Byron, who died while Byron was in Greece.

Stanzas. Published with *Childe Harold's Pilgrimage. A Romaunt* (1812), second edition. An elegy for John Edleston.

epigraph. Quoting Shenstone's Inscription 'On an Ornamented Urn' (trans.: 'Alas, how much less it matters to socialize with others than to remember you').

3 l. 24. *Nor age can chill*: cf. *Antony and Cleopatra* II. ii. 240.

l. 39. *untimely snatch'd*: cf. *Macbeth* V. viii. 16.

l. 45. *foul from fair*: cf. *Macbeth* I. i. 11.

5 from *Childe Harold's Pilgrimage*. Byron left England for Portugal on 2 July 1809. The first two cantos of this poem, which established Byron's fame, were written in 1809–10 when his travels had taken him to the Levant, and were published in March 1812. They constitute a radical transformation of the popular genre of travelogue known as the topographical poem. Byron interiorizes the form so drastically that it mutates into a drama of personal history. The historical context in which the personal record is set is turned to a reflection of Byron's own psychological condition. This is true of all four cantos of the poem. In 1816, after he exiled himself from England, Byron resumed the poem with the third canto, which was published the same year. He wrote Canto IV a year later, in Italy, and it was published in 1818. The two later cantos were consciously written against the background of the defeat of Napoleon and the restoration of the monarchies in 1814–15. The whole comprises an autobiographical journey into and through a deep personal malaise which Byron represents as a symbol of the condition of Europe between 1809 and 1818.

Byron's itinerary in Cantos I–II takes him to Portugal and Spain, where the Peninsular War erupted in 1808 following Napoleon's invasion of the Iberian peninsula in 1807, the revolt of Spain in May 1808, and the arrival of English troops in August 1808. Byron left Spain for Gibraltar on 3 August 1809, then went to Malta where he had a brief affair with Constance Spencer Smith, and then left for Albania at the end of September. In December he went to Athens, which became his base for the next year and a half's travels throughout the Levant. In Canto III the time scheme is much more brief: it narrates Byron's movements from his departure from England in April 1816 to his arrival in Geneva in June, where he met Shelley. Canto IV, the only canto which is entirely recollective, narrates Byron's trip (April–May 1817) from Venice by way of Ferrara and Florence to Rome; it was composed July–December 1817.

5 l. 4. Byron is thinking of the partial destruction of the Acropolis (in 1687) during the struggle between Turkey and Venice for control of Greece.

l. 19. *Son of the morning*: a Levantine.

6 l. 55. *thou*: Socrates.

8 *The Giaour*. As the Advertisement suggests, this poem is set in Greece shortly after 1779, when Hassan Ghazi broke the rebellion of the Arnauts in the Morea. Byron does not have any specific event in mind, but rather means to call up the general state of Greece under Ottoman rule at the end of the eighteenth century. Though sometimes read as a mere adventure story ornamented with 'Eastern imagery', the poem is in fact a displaced critique of current European ideology. The allegorical character of the tale is clear when one reads it in the context of Cantos I–II of *Childe Harold*. Byron wrote the poem in late 1812 and early 1813; it was published in 1813 and created nearly as great a sensation as his previous publication *Childe Harold*. It went through fourteen editions in two years, and it gradually grew from a 1st edn. of 684 lines to its final form in the 7th edn. Part of the sensationalism of the poem rested on the belief, which Byron did not discourage, that the narrative was based upon events in which Byron himself took part. The poem is the first in the series of famous 'Byronic Tales' which Byron was soon to produce. Particular notice should be taken of Byron's inimitable notes, which supply a peculiar ionic vantage on the heroic tragedy narrated in the verse.

8–13 ll. 1–167. Not part of the 'Turkish Tale' proper; the point of view here is, like Byron's, contemporary and English.

9 l. 9. *Colonna*: Cape Sunium.

13 l. 177. *Port Leone*: the ancient Piraeus.

l. 190. *Giaour*. The 'g' is pronounced soft, as 'j'; hence the word is sounded 'jowr'.

22 l. 528. *Parne*: Parnassus.

23 l. 566. *Liakura*: Parnassus.

43 *Byron's Notes to The Giaour*. l. 3. *Themistocles*: early fifth-century BC Greek hero and statesman, celebrated for his part in the struggle against the Persian invasion.

44 l. 225. *Bairam*: three-day festival at the end of the month of Ramadhan.

45 l. 434. *Felo de se*: a felon on himself (i.e. a suicide). *Catos*: Cato the Younger (95–46 BC), a byword of the noble suicide.

l. 479. *first editions*: Editions 1–4 of the poem; this and the next sentence were added in the 5th edn. *d'Herbelot*: Barthélemy d'Herbelot, in his *Bibliothèque orientale* (1697). *Richardson*: John Richardson, *Dictionary of Persian, Arabic, and English* (1777).

l. 483. *'facilis . . . Averni'*. The descent to hell is easy' (Virgil, *Aeneid*, VI. 26).

l. 494. *'plus . . . Arabie'*. 'More Arab than in Arabia.'

l. 593. *Capitan Pacha*: Ali Pacha: 'the lion of Yannina', quasi-independent governor of the Turkish dominions of Albania and most of Epirus from 1787 to 1820.

46 l. 755. *Tournefort . . . Thalaba*: Joseph Pitton de Tournefort's *Relation d'un voyage du Levant* (1717), quoted in Robert Southey's *Thalaba the Destroyer* (1801), the notes to Book 8. *Arsenius*. Bishop of Monembasia (c. 1530).

47 l. 1077. *Tahiri, Basili*: Byron's Albanian servants; for the incident see Marchand, *Byron's Letters and Journals*, II. 30–1, 'Palao-castro': modern Greek for 'old fortress'. *'villainous company'*, *1 Henry IV*, III. iii. 10.

48 l. 1334. *Muchtar Pacha*: Ali Pacha's eldest son. *Weber . . . Vathek*. Henry Weber in his *Tales of the East* (1812) comments on William Beckford's *Vathek* (1786), which heavily influenced Byron's poem. *Rasselas . . . Eblis*. Byron refers to Samuel Johnson's eastern tale *Rasselas* (1759) and to the fabulous Hall of Eblis in *Vathek*.

49 from *The Corsair*. These selections from *The Corsair* (1814) and the next poem in this edition, *Lara* (1814), are printed in order to illustrate the character of the so-called Byronic Hero. Such a figure, appearing throughout Byron's works, is one of the poet's signal legacies to culture. Variants of this symbolic person—a proud, gloomy, and doomed figure of aristocratic heritage—proliferated throughout the art and literature of the West, especially in the nineteenth century. It goes without saying that readers have, from the first, identified Byron with this (anti-)hero. Byron of course disclaimed the identification even as his life and works repeatedly encouraged it. The Byronic hero focuses and symbolizes an experience of psychic and social despair.

Antithetical to every form of instituted culture and authority, he attaches himself only to an idealized (female) love object. The final couplet of *The Corsair* neatly summarizes his career: 'He left a Corsair's name to other times, / Linked with one virtue, and a thousand crimes.'

52 from *Lara*. See previous note.

54 *Stanzas for Music*. Written early in May 1814; the subject is Byron's half-sister Augusta. Unpublished in Byron's lifetime.

55 *They Say that Hope is Happiness*. Published after Byron's death.

epigraph. *Georgics* II. 490 (trans.: 'Happy is the person who can understand the causes of things').

56 *Stanzas for Music*. First published in 1815 with musical score. The poem is an elegy for the Duke of Dorset, one of Byron's boyhood friends.

epigraph. (trans.: 'O fount of tears, that have their sacred sources in the tender spirit; four times blessed is he who has felt you, holy nymph, gushing forth from the depths of his heart.')

57 *She Walks in Beauty*. Published in Byron's *Hebrew Melodies* (1815). Written about Byron's cousin Anne Wilmot, whom he saw at a London party in June 1814.

58 *Sun of the Sleepless!* Another *Hebrew Melody*, the poem is Byron's remarkable commentary on the moon as the 'star' of the romantic imagination.

The Destruction of Semnacherib. Another *Hebrew Melody*; the text is 2 Kgs. 19 and Isa. 37.

59 *When We Two Parted*. Published in Byron's *Poems* (1816) but written earlier. Byron is recalling two women: Lady Frances Wedderburn Webster, with whom he had a brief 'platonic' affair in 1813; and Lady Caroline Lamb.

61 *Fare Thee Well!* Written late Mar. 1816 and printed (fifty copies for private circulation) 8 Apr. 1816. Thereafter the poem was picked up by the periodical press and widely disseminated, as Byron no doubt knew it would be. Written to Byron's estranged wife, the poem has always been one of his most celebrated—not to say notorious. It is best read not as a love poem but as a sly move in the game of the Separation. It is, ultimately, a cruel (as well as cruelly self-deceived) poem, masking its aims under the rhetoric of a repentant but loving husband.

63 [*A Fragment*]. Unpublished in Byron's lifetime; written July 1816.

64 *Prometheus*. Published in 1817 in *The Prisoner of Chillon and Other Poems*; written summer 1816.

66 *Stanzas to [Augusta]*. Written July 1816; published with the foregoing poem. This is Byron's public self-judgement following the break-up of his marriage, the ensuing scandal, and his self-exile.

67 *[Epistle to Augusta]*. Unpublished in Byron's lifetime; written Aug. 1816.

68 l. 15. *grandsire*: Admiral John Byron (1723–86).

71 l. 128. *tie*: the blood-tie to Augusta, as opposed to the marriage tie to his wife.

72 *Darkness*. Published with 'Prometheus' (above); written summer 1816.

73 l. 50. *clung*: shrivelled (obsolete usage).

74 from *Childe Harold's Pilgrimage. Canto III*. See general note above for Cantos I–II.

l. 6. *apples on the Dead Sea's shore*: Fabled to be 'fair without, and within ashes' (Byron's note).

l. 11. *tale*: both 'story' and 'counting'.

l. 19. *greatest . . . of men*: Napoleon.

77 l. 109. Rousseau was born (1712) in Geneva, which is where Byron is writing.

78 l. 127. Julie, the heroine of Rousseau's novel of that name (1761), which influenced the leaders of the French Revolution.

l. 135. Byron's note to this passage recalls Rousseau's *Confessions* where he narrates 'his passion for the Comptesse d'Houdetot . . . and his long walk every morning for the sake of the single kiss which was the common salutation of French acquaintance'.

l. 147. *world in flame*: The French Revolution.

81 l. 232. *Cytherea's zone*: The cincture of Aphrodite, which gave the wearer the power to attract love.

82 l. 244. Byron's note identifies this as a midnight storm breaking over the Jura on 13 June 1816.

84 from *Manfred*. Published 1817; composed largely in the summer of 1816. This is Byron's most Nietzschean work: an exploration of the meaning, and even the possibility, of integrity and selfhood. Byron's debt to Goethe's *Faust* Part I is evident, although Byron's play picks up where Goethe's left off.

epigraph: *Hamlet* I. v. 166–7.

l. 9. *grief . . . wise*: cf. Eccles. 1: 18.

ll. 10–12. See Gen. 2–3.

89 l. 175. *face to face*: cf. Exod. 33: 11.

l. 192 ff. Byron published this lyric separately in 1817 under the title 'The Incantation', as a thinly disguised curse upon his estranged wife.

92 [*So, We'll Go No More a Roving*]. Unpublished by Byron; sent in a letter to Thomas Moore, 28 Feb. 1817. Byron is thinking of the Venetian carnival, just ended, as well as his gay life in London during his Years of Fame before he left England.

92 from *Beppo*. Published early in 1818, *Beppo*'s *ottava rima* forecasts Byron's masterwork *Don Juan*.

94 l. 35. *Monmouth-street . . . Rag Fair*: Centres for second-hand clothes.

l. 63. Harvey, a popular fish sauce.

95 l. 91. *That picture*: 'Triple Portrait', attributed to Giorgione but actually by Titian.

96 l. 112. *lost Pleiad*: Merope, one of the seven Pleiades; her star was dim because she married a mortal.

97 l. 129. *becaficas*: song birds; a culinary delicacy.

l. 155. Byron's note to this line cites Vasari's *Life* of Raphael, where it is reported that an unusually heavy bout of lovemaking weakened the painter's constitution shortly before his death.

98 l. 166. Habeas corpus was suspended in 1817, restored in 1818.

l. 183. *glories*: most particularly, Waterloo.

99 l. 193. Ironically self-referential; Byron recalls his famous 'Oriental Tales' like *The Giaour*, *The Corsair*, *Lara*, etc.

100 from *Childe Harold's Pilgrimage, Canto IV*. See above for general note on the poem.

l. 1. *Bridge of Sighs*: The Ponte dei Sospiri separating the Doge's palace from the state prison.

101 l. 34. *Pierre*: a character in Thomas Otway's *Venice Preserved* (1682).

103 l. 106. *base pageant*: the Congress of Vienna (Sept. 1815).

l. 116. *North*: England.

l. 118. *tower*: the tomb of Cecilia Metella, on the Appian Way. Byron means to contrast her with his estranged wife.

110 l. 319. *upas*: legendary tree of Java which poisoned the surrounding earth.

111 ll. 353 ff. The Canto's most explicit autobiographical passage.

113 l. 433. *here*: the Colosseum.

114 l. 457. Byron's note to the passage refers to Rome's brutal gladiatorial spectacles.

117 l. 559. This stanza and the next comment on two famous statues in

the Museo Pio-Clementino, the Laocoon and the Apollo Belvedere.

120 *To the Po.* Unpublished in Byron's lifetime; the poem deals with Byron's love for his 'last attachment', the Contessa Teresa Guiccioli.

121 [*Stanzas*]. Unpublished in Byron's lifetime, this is another poem reflecting on Byron's love for the Contessa Guiccioli.

124 *Don Juan.* Byron started his masterwork early in July 1818 with no intention of writing what would finally become the most comprehensive epic of his age, and arguably the greatest English poem since *Paradise Lost.* As he told Murray on 12 Aug. 1819, he 'had no plan' for his poem. His initial aim was merely to write another work in the style of *Beppo*, but with more bite in the attack upon the dominant literary modes of the day (epitomized for Byron in the conservative Lakist group of Robert Southey, Wordsworth, and Coleridge), and with an explicit assault upon the politics and ideology of England and Europe in the period of the restored thrones. These aims carried him through the first five cantos (Cantos I–II were published together in 1819, and Cantos III–V together in 1821). But opposition to his poem stiffened back in England, and his enthusiasm cooled at the lack of encouragement, especially from his publisher and friends. Byron stopped the poem at the end of 1820 and did not resume it again until early in 1821. In that interim, however, the poem underwent a drastic act of reconception. Not only did Byron hit upon a plan for the narrative level of the poem; he also provided the epic with a clear tripartite historical structure: at the story level, Juan's career (which begins, in the poem, in 1789, and which was to end on the guillotine in 1792 or 1793); at the narrative level, the precise epoch of Byron's act of narrating his poem and producing its texts (1818–24, or the period of the entrenched Restoration); and at the memorial or recollective level, the London years of Byron's rise to fame and plunge into disgrace. In *Don Juan* each of these levels is made to comment upon the others, and the entire poem offers itself as a massive act of social and historical interpretation: a poetically grounded explanation of the meaning of the period 1789–1824.

This reconception was signalled by a change of publishers. Cantos VI–XVI were published in four separate volumes in 1823–4 by the radical publisher John Hunt. It was also signalled by some noticeable changes in the poem's style. First, the famous digressive manner becomes more closely integrated into the narrative of the story (in the early cantos the digressions tend to be offered as set-piece units). Second, the poem's radical politics become more flagrant ('it is necessary, in the present clash of philosophy and tyranny', he said in 1821, as he resumed work on his poem, 'to throw away the scabbard. I know it is against fearful odds; but the battle must be fought'). Third, the episodic character of the early *Don Juan* succeeds to a much more integrated narrative—to what has in fact been called, with some justice, a 'novel in verse'.

Don Juan is a poem that must be read in the context of Byron's life and his age ('Almost all Don Juan is *real* life—either my own—or from people I knew'). It was begun at the same time as his famous *Memoirs* (which were burned after his death), and consciously initiated as an ironic alternative to Coleridge's reactionary *Biographia Literaria* (1817). Running through the poem is not only a series of open commentaries on contemporary people and events, but also a set of coded biographical allusions meant for those whom he liked to call 'the knowing ones'. (In one of the poem's most astonishing acts of wit (Canto XIV, sts. 21–2), Byron encodes a reference to his codes.) As a result, the reader of the poem needs to be somewhat familiar with its *dramatis personae*: Byron's loves, friends, acquaintances, and especially his enemies. The notes below, it is hoped, will help somewhat in this regard. Also important to see is that the poem maintains a systematic parody of the epic and its conventions, and that its conversational style is in the (classical) tradition of Horace, in the (Italian) tradition of Boiardo, Pulci, Berni, and Casti, and in the (English) tradition of verse like that of Rochester and Pope, and of prose like that of Smollett, Sterne, and Fielding.

124 *epigraph*. 'It is difficult to personalize general subjects.'

Dedication: l. 24. *adry*, *Bob*: a 'dry bob' is slang for coition without emission.

125 l. 46. Wordsworth's place may be in the Customs: it is, I think, in that of the Excise; besides another at Lord Lonsdale's table, where this poetical charlatan and political parasite picks up the crums [*sic*] with a hardened alacrity, the converted Jacobin having long subsided into the clownish sycophant of the worst prejudices of aristocracy. (Byron)

126 l. 86. 'Pale, but not cadaverous.' Milton's two elder daughters are said to have robbed him of his books, besides cheating and plaguing him in the economy of his house, etc. Hayley compares him to Lear. (Byron)

l. 88. *Castlereagh*: Robert Stewart, Viscount Castlereagh (1769–1822), the Foreign Secretary and chief architect of England's Restoration policies. Byron's animus against him has its origin in what Byron regarded as Castlereagh's betrayal of Ireland to English and aristocratic interests, and it did not abate even when Byron learned of Castlereagh's suicide.

127 l. 117. *Eutropius*: a eunuch in the Eastern (Roman) Empire who was raised to high office.

128 l. 132. '*buff and blue*': the colours of the Whig Club.

l. 136. I allude not to our friend Landor's hero, the traitor Count Julian, but to Gibbon's hero, vulgarly yclept 'The Apostate'. (Byron)

Canto I, [*Julia and Juan*]. This is the central passage of the first canto. Julia, the young wife of old Don Alfonso, and Juan play out Byron's version of Dante's Paolo and Francesca episode, from the *Inferno*.

141 l. 414. The motto on one of Byron's seals (trans.: 'She follows you everywhere').

142 *Canto III*, [*Haidée's and Juan's Feast*]. Juan's affair with Julia ending in disaster, he leaves Spain, is shipwrecked, and then washes up on a remote Greek island where he meets Haidée, the beautiful daughter of the pirate Lambro, who is meanwhile away from the island.

144 l. 90. *a poet*: this figure recalls Demodocus, the court poet of the *Odyssey*; but the contemporary references are to the reactionary Southey and (Southey's opposite) Byron himself.

145 l. 114. Horace's inspired poet.

l. 121. *trimmer*: one who plays both sides in politics.

147 l. 158. *de Staël*: in her study *De l'Allemagne* (1810).

l. 159. '*Trecentisti*': Italian writers of the fourteenth century.

l. 167. *Scian . . . Teian muse*: Homer and Anacreon, respectively; the poetry of war and the poetry of love.

l. 179. *king*: Xerxes watching the battle of Salamis.

149 l. 219. The legendary Cadmus gave writing to the Greeks.

l. 224. Anacreon served the tyrant of Samos, Polycrates.

l. 238. *Heracleidan*: descendants of Hercules.

l. 239. *Franks*: Europeans.

151 l. 306. Southey planned to establish a Utopian Communist community in America.

152 l. 307. Wordsworth had a tax-collecting sinecure from the government.

l. 312. Coleridge and Southey married the Fricker sisters (who were not milliners).

l. 324. Joanna Southcott (1750–1814), religious millinarian.

153 *Canto IV*, [*The Death of Haidée*]. Juan's island idyl with Haidée ends when Lambro returns; Juan is sold into slavery and Haidée goes mad and dies.

157 *Canto XI*. l. 1. *Bishop Berkeley*. What follows is a materialist critique of George Berkeley's philosophical idealism.

158 l. 18. '*dainty Ariel*': *The Tempest*, v. i. 95.

161 l. 109. *the Moon's late minion*: see *1 Henry IV*, I. ii. 25.

l. 122. *got my gruel*: killed.

l. 123. *max*: gin.

l. 133. *kiddy*: dandified street thief.

l. 135. *Full flash*: knowing, not easily fooled.

162 l. 139. '*Crowner's 'quest*': coroner's inquest (*Hamlet*, v. i. 21).

st. 19. The advance of science and of language has rendered it unnecessary to translate the above good and true English, spoken in its original purity by the select mobility and their patrons. The following is a stanza of a song which was very popular, at least in my early days:—

> On the high toby-spice flash the muzzle,
>   In spite of each gallows old scout;
> If you at the spellken can't hustle,
>   You'll be hobbled in making a Clout.
>
> Then your Blowing will wax gallows haughty,
>   When she hears of your scaly mistake,
> She'll surely turn snitch for the forty,
>   That her Jack may be regular weight.

If there be any Gemman so ignorant as to require a traduction, I refer him to my old friend and corporeal pastor and master, John Jackson, Esq., Professor of Pugilism; who I trust still retains the strength and symmetry of his model of a form, together with his good humour, and athletic as well as mental accomplishments. (Byron)

162 l. 162. *Like . . . light*: See Canto VI, st. 55.

163 l. 171. '*purl*': hot gin and beer.

l. 176. Gas lights were introduced in 1812 in London.

164 l. 208. During the French Revolution, some were hanged from lampposts.

l. 232. 'Hells', gaming-houses. What their number may now be in this life, I know not. Before I was of age I knew them pretty accurately, both 'gold' and 'silver'. I was once nearly called out by an acquaintance because, when he asked me where I thought that his soul would be found hereafter, I answered, 'In Silver Hell'. (Byron)

168 l. 340. 'Anent' was a Scottish phrase, meaning 'concerning'—'with regard to'. It has been made English by the Scotch Novels; and as the Frenchman said—'If it *be not, ought to be* English.' (Byron)

st. 45. Here begins Byron's representation of the fashionable world which he knew in his Years of Fame (1812–15).

169 l. 373. '*flaws or starts*': *Macbeth*, III. iv. 63.

l. 385. 'Drapery Misses'. This term is probably any thing now but a *mystery*. It was however almost so to me when I first returned from the East in 1811–12. It means a pretty, a highborn, a fashionable young female, well instructed by her friends, and furnished by her milliner with a wardrobe upon credit, to be repaid, when *married*, by the *husband*. The riddle was first read to me by a young and pretty heiress, on my praising the 'drapery' of an '*untochered*' but 'pretty virginities' (like Mrs Anne Page) of the *then* day, which has now been some years yesterday:—she assured me that the thing was common in London; and as her own thousands, and blooming looks, and rich simplicity of array, put any suspicion in her own case out of the question, I confess I gave some credit to the allegation. If necessary, authorities might be cited, in which case I could quote both 'drapery' and the wearers. Let us hope, however, that it is now obsolete. (Byron)

170 l. 402. *Drawcansir*: the braggart hero in George Villiers' *The Rehearsal* (1671).

l. 413. A notional character; typifies a bluestocking.

171 l. 427. *Banquo's glass*: *Macbeth*, IV. i. 112–22.

ll. 441–2. Napoleon's retreat from Moscow (1812), defeat at Leipzig (1813), and disaster at Waterloo (1814, epitomized by the crucial action at Mont St Jean).

l. 443. '*La Belle Alliance*': the Quadruple Alliance of England, Austria, Prussia, Russia.

l. 448. *Lowe*: Sir Hudson Lowe, governor of St Helena during Napoleon's imprisonment.

l. 454. *reverend Cambyses Croly*: Revd. George Croly, minor literary figure.

l. 456: '*by these Hilts*': *1 Henry IV*, II. iv. 197.

st. 58. The subject is Henry Hart Milman, minor poet and historian.

172 l. 465. *Euphues*: Bryan Proctor ('Barry Cornwall').

l. 473. This myth of Keats's death is founded on the savage *Quarterly Review* article by John Wilson Croker in 1818.

ll. 487–8. *the thirty . . . tyrants*: the Thirty Tyrants during the reign of Gallienus in the third century.

173 l. 491. '*dreadful trade*' . . . '*gathers samphire*': *King Lear*, IV. vi. 15.

l. 516. To cure him of his unfaithfulness, Deïaneira gave Hercules a shirt dipped in the blood of the centaur Nessus; it killed him.

174 l. 536. '*Or Molu*': gilded bronze furniture decorations, popular in the Regency.

175 l. 572. *bogle*: goblin.

176 l. 590. '*rack and manger*': waste and destruction.

l. 598. i.e. between Tories and Whigs.

l. 601. This is the theme of Edward Young's *Resignation* (1762), published when he was 80.

l. 603. *eight years past*: 1814, the height of Byron's Years of Fame.

ll. 607–8. The lines define the persons named in the next few stanzas, people Byron knew during his Years of Fame.

l. 615. *Five per Cents*: the interest from investment securities in the Public Funds.

177 l. 619. George III made two wills (1770, 1810) but he left the second unsigned.

l. 620. '*Fum*': George IV; Byron alludes immediately below to the king's trip to Scotland in 1822.

l. 622. Sawney is a derisive nickname for a Scotsman.

l. 623. '*Caw . . . thee*'. 'You scratch me, I'll scratch you.'

l. 631. George Grenville (1712–70), a supporter of Pitt, later turned against him; his son, William Wyndham, Baron Grenville (1759–1834) turned from a reformer to a Tory later in his career.

l. 633. Byron glances at his former liaisons with Lady Caroline Lamb and Lady Frances Wedderburn Webster.

178 l. 658. *Duke*: Wellington.

l. 661. '*blue Peter*': nautical flag signalling departure.

l. 670. *Congress*: the Congress of Verona (1822).

l. 675. *the Funds*: see above, l. 615, and n.

l. 676. *squeakers*. Byron derides the loss of authority of the landed aristocracy.

l. 679. '*thin potations*': *2 Henry IV*, IV. iii. 133.

179 ll. 684–5. '*Life's . . . villains*': *Macbeth*, v. v. 24 and *1 Henry IV*, II. iv. 539.

l. 693. *Atalantis*: Mrs Mary Manley's scandalous novel known popularly as *The New Atalantis* (1709).

180 *Canto XIV*

184 l. 143. '*ci-devant jeunes hommes*': young men of former days.

185 ll. 161–2. Freely adapting Virgil, *Aeneid* II. 6, 91: 'I speak of what I am familiar with; these are trifles in which I played a small part.'

186 *Canto XV*, [*Dinner at the Amundeville Estate*]. Juan is in England as a Russian envoy.

l. 9. *Miss Millpond*: cf. Byron's wife's maiden name, Annabella Milbanke. The portrait here fits her.

l. 19. *star or bluestring*: i.e. on a man with a royal decoration such as the Order of the Garter.

188 ll. 73–5. Tiberius forbade the busts of Brutus and Cassius at the funeral of Junia, Cassius' wife; but Tacitus says that the absence only made people more aware of them.

189 l. 111. '*Anthony's by Caesar*': see *Macbeth*, III. i. 55–7.

191 l. 155. '*I sound my Warison*': *The Lay of the Last Minstrel*, IV. xxiv.

ll. 177 ff. Byron takes most of the details of this dinner from Louis Ude's famous *The French Cook* (1813).

192 l. 203. *young Ammon*: Alexander the Great.

l. 206. *Apicius*: Roman epicure.

l. 210. The rhyme is wrong.

l. 215. A dish 'à la Lucullus'. This hero, who conquered the East, has left his more extended celebrity to the transplantation of cherries (which he first brought to Europe) and the nomenclature of some very good dishes;—and I am not sure that (barring indigestion) he has not done more service to mankind by his cookery than by his conquests. A cherry-tree may weigh against a bloody quarrel: besides, he has contrived to earn celebrity from both. (Byron)

193 l. 232. Byron's note identifies these cream puffs garnished with jam as 'part of the flank for the second course', as set forth in Ude.

l. 245. *springald*: a young man (archaic).

ll. 249–50. *gibier . . . salmi*: game and game stew.

194 l. 254. '*Bubble and squeak*': fried beef and cabbage.

l. 256. '*Becasse*': woodcock.

197 l. 354. *Nem. con.*: unanimously.

l. 355. *crim. con.*: here, adultery.

l. 376. Subauditur '*Non*'; omitted for the sake of euphony. (Byron)

199 *Francesca of Rimini*. Unpublished in Byron's lifetime.

l. 11. *Caina*: the ninth circle of hell.

l. 15. *the bard*: Virgil, who is guiding Dante through hell.

200 l. 27. Virgil 'knows' because he is prevented from entering Paradise because he is unbaptized.

from *Cain*. Published 1821 with two other plays, *Sardanapalus* and *The Two Foscari*. *Cain* caused an immense controversy when it appeared. The excerpt here is one of the most eloquent statements of intellectual freedom in the language.

202 [*Thoughts on Freedom*]. The manuscript of this fragment was found among Byron's papers at Albaro after he left Italy for Greece in 1823.

On This Day I Complete My Thirty-Sixth Year. Written Messalonghi. 22 January 1824, shortly before Byron's death; the poem was written with Loukas Chalandritsanos in mind, a Greek youth who was with Byron in his final days in Greece.

203 l. 23. Byron's note: 'The slain were borne on their shields. Witness the Spartan mother's speech to her son, delivered with his buckler: "either *with* this or *on* this".'

Further Reading

EDITIONS

Jerome J. McGann, ed., *Byron. The Complete Poetical Works* (Vols. i–vii 1980–93)

Leslie A. Marchand, ed., *Byron's Letters and Journals* (12 vols., 1975–82)

T. G. Steffan, E. Steffan, and W. W. Pratt, eds., *Lord Byron. Don Juan* (revised, with additions, 1982)

CRITICAL AND BIOGRAPHICAL STUDIES

Anne Barton, *Byron: "Don Juan"* (1992)

Elizabeth Boyd, *Byron's Don Juan* (1945)

Jerome Christensen, *Lord Byron's Strength: Romantic Writing and Commercial Society* (1992)

Michael Cooke, *The Blind Man Traces the Circle* (1969)

Robert Gleckner, *Byron and the Ruins of Paradise* (1967)

—— ed., *Critical Essays on Lord Byron* (1991)

M. K. Joseph, *Byron the Poet* (1964)

Alice Levine and Robert N. Keane, ed., *Rereading Byron* (1993)

Peter Manning, *Byron and His Fictions* (1978)

Leslie A. Marchand, *Byron. A Biography* (3 vols., 1958)

Jerome J. McGann, *Fiery Dust. Byron's Poetic Development* (1968)

—— *Don Juan in Context* (1976)

Doris Langley Moore, *The Late Lord Byron* (1961)

Iris Origo, *The Last Attachment* (1949)

Andrew Rutherford, *Byron. A Critical Study* (1961)

—— *Byron. The Critical Heritage* (1970)

—— ed., *Byron, Augustan and Romantic* (1990)

Index of Titles and First Lines

OXFORD POETRY LIBRARY

WILLIAM WORDSWORTH

Edited by Stephen Gill and Duncan Wu

Wordsworth was one of the most illustrious of the Romantic poets. In this selection generous extracts are given from his important work *The Prelude*, together with many of his shorter poems. The reader will find classics such as *Tintern Abbey*, *Westminster Bridge* and 'I wandered lonely as a cloud' well represented. Notes and introduction are provided by Wordsworth's biographers, Stephen Gill and Duncan Wu.

OXFORD POETRY LIBRARY

ALEXANDER POPE

Edited by Pat Rogers

Pope has been acknowledged as the most important poet of the first half of the eighteenth century. This selection includes his brilliant poems *An Essay on Criticism*, *Windsor Forest*, and his masterpiece of social satire, *The Rape of the Lock*. Together with a representative sample of Pope's other verse, Pat Rogers gives an eloquent defence of Pope's poetic practice.

OXFORD POETRY LIBRARY

SAMUEL TAYLOR COLERIDGE

Edited by Heather Jackson

Coleridge was one of the most significant figures in the development of Romantic poetry. This new selection represents the full range of his poetic gifts, from his early polemic poetry such as the *Sonnets on Eminent Characters*, to the maturity of the blank verse poems, *Fears in Solitude* and *Frost at Midnight*. Also included are the wonderful works, *Kubla Khan* and *The Rime of the Ancient Mariner*.

OXFORD POETRY LIBRARY
JOHN DRYDEN
Edited by Keith Walker

Dryden was the leading poet of his day, and dominated the literary scene with satires such as *MacFlecknoe* and *Absalom and Achitophel*. This selection represents the full range of his talent and pays particular attention to his classical translations, which gave new life to English verse. These include extracts from Horace, Lucretius, Ovid, and Virgil's *Aeneid*, as well as his own fables and reworkings of some of Chaucer's tales.

OXFORD POETRY LIBRARY

SIR PHILIP SIDNEY

Edited by Katherine Duncan-Jones

Sidney, a contemporary of Shakespeare, is now considered to be one of the most important poets of the Elizabethan era. In addition to a number of shorter lyrics, this selection by a leading Sidney scholar includes his most substantial works *The Defence of Poesy*, *The New Arcadia*, and *Astrophil and Stella*, the first sonnet sequence ever written in English.

OXFORD POETRY LIBRARY
THOMAS HARDY
Edited by Samuel Hayes

Thomas Hardy continues to be one of the best loved of the great English poets. His enduring popularity is perhaps due to the universality of his subject matter: birth, childhood, love, marriage, age, death. These subjects are well represented in this selection which contains poems taken from all eight of Hardy's poetry volumes.

OXFORD POETRY LIBRARY

ANDREW MARVELL

Edited by Keith Walker and Frank Kermode

Marvell is regarded as one of the finest Metaphysical poets. His brilliant use of conceits and luxuriant imagery is ever-present in this selection which includes much of his lyrical poetry together with some of his more political works. Such famous poems as *To his Coy Mistress*, the Mower poems, and *On a Drop of Dew* can all be found, with informative notes and introduction by Frank Kermode and Keith Walker.